THE EDITOR OF "THE GREATER WORLD"
28-2-85.

Journey into Light

Journey into Light

An account of forty years'
communication with a brother
in the After Life

RUTH PLANT

CASSELL · LONDON

CASSELL & COMPANY LTD
35 Red Lion Square, London WC1R 4SG
Sydney, Auckland
Toronto, Johannesburg

First published 1972

I.S.B.N. 0 304 93864 5

Printed in Great Britain by
The Camelot Press Ltd., London and Southampton

F. 872

Foreword

As one of the daughters of Sir Oliver Lodge, who plays such a prominent part in the pages of this book, and who indeed recommended that well-known medium Mrs Osborne Leonard to Miss Ruth Plant when she lost her brother so tragically, I feel a particular pleasure in being asked to contribute this Foreword.

Journey into Light is a book which will be of considerable help and should give great comfort to anyone who has been bereaved. But it also contains much else of interest and information. Its horizons are broad, and it will prove a valuable asset to those who wish to see beyond the veil which divides this world from the next—a veil which is growing thin and which one day, we may hope, will disappear.

BARBARA GODLEE

To Gladys Osborne Leonard

Who came to our aid in our loss and helped us to gain a whole new world

Contents

Introduction

This book has been created by circumstances and events, not only by individual choice. It was first suggested that I should write it because I had some interesting records of communications from the After Life which came chiefly through Mrs Osborne Leonard, a famous medium who had worked with Sir Oliver Lodge, and which had not so far been made known. I did not then see the immediate relation these had to current problems today. Most work which is destined to be done—and I do believe that there is a plan connecting our individual tasks with the needs of the community—has its full purpose only made known to us as the work goes on; its timing in the scheme of things is beyond our arrangement.

While great progress has been made in the sphere of earthly communications, offering people, especially the young, faster and more efficient ways of reaching their destinations, we have not progressed at a similar rate in our discoveries relating to the Unseen world.

Many people today are criticized for their impatience to alter the existing order of things, the frustration of which has produced a pattern of articulate protest within communal groups. Those who make this criticism are failing to comprehend the situation as a whole, and the limitations of present horizons, in an age becoming subconsciously aware of a far vaster scheme of things beyond our normal earthly view in both spiritual and scientific fields.

Some who have grown up in inherited disciplines to which they are attuned, or who are endowed with special gifts for assimilating influences from higher sources, have moved forward, and thus considerable upheavals have begun in the orthodox Churches.

A majority, however, remains totally unequipped for any

journey beyond the earthly sphere. Many content themselves with absorption in the present through interest in earthly belongings, hobbies, and so forth, while others face the bitter reality of a life without a faith and occupy themselves with excitement and gaiety, justified by the tenet 'eat drink and be merry for tomorrow you die'.

Earlier in the present century certain explorations were made into the world beyond the veil by such men of international standing as Sir Oliver Lodge, Lord Balfour and Sir Arthur Conan Doyle, and some considerable progress was achieved. These inquiries were precipitated by the carnage that took place during the First World War when Sir Oliver Lodge's own son Raymond was killed in action and many other young men like him passed into the Unseen.

The men who carried out these experiments were a group of scientists and intellectuals respected for their individual reputation and integrity rather than for their psychic discoveries. The time was not ready for a wide acceptance of their ideas. The ordinary scientist would not then admit the possibility of inhabited planets elsewhere in our galaxy or of states of consciousness beyond his knowing, as most would today. The golden age of psychic research therefore flowered and faded with the passing of the individuals concerned and without any effective roots being established.

The inquiry into life after death, in what might be called a more domestic form, has, however, been continually carried on by the Spiritualists through their many Churches. They have ministered faithfully to those who have turned to them in some great personal bereavement, seeking contact with an individual loved one. Some of these seekers have compiled books containing records of considerable value. But, on the whole, the gap has widened in recent years between Spiritualists and psychic researchers, the latter having become somewhat preoccupied with the investigations of extra-sensory perception and the testing of telepathy between subjects on earth.

On the other hand, many scientists were attracted by the fascinating fields for research opened up by the work of the great psychologists, Freud, Jung and Adler, through the analysis of the individual subconscious, and from this interest came the later developments of group and depth psychology. So today the road has begun to lead back once more to the absorbing questions of the Unseen.

A new social problem, the taking of drugs by young people, superficially attributed to boredom and a wish for 'kicks', is, I believe, born of a desire to probe the unconscious, to find a meaning for life beyond the possession of mere material objects, of which they have an abundance. Their actions are a response to the group consciousness of this age, a reaching out towards the destined path of their particular generation to explore the unseen at the different levels of consciousness at which man can operate. They are the avant garde of the new age, but like early aviators they have not yet found the right vehicle for making themselves airborne and are apt to crash near the ground.

This book is mainly about the efforts of a normally intelligent young man—a medical student, my brother—for whose integrity I can vouch, to get through to us from the Unseen after his sudden death. He succeeded in bridging the gap between the two worlds through a sensitive who had trained and disciplined herself by years of unstinted devotion to her profession, and who had created a system for this work which is a valuable source of study. When choosing from the great store of records in my possession I have tried to select those concerned with the technical details of linking up so far as we know them, and indicate some suppositions for future investigation. I have tried to emphasize how we must play our own part if we are to receive information correctly, and how, if we succeed, we will find the information fitting into a pattern of our own lives. This can give us guidance and direction, provided we wait for future events to work out at the proper moment. Then we can follow the intended pattern.

My approach may seem mundane to those who have sought revelation through the use of exotic drugs. But it will prove to be a more sure and more creative foundation: and not only in the personal sense, for I believe that ultimately this world and the Unseen will become one. It may also seem inadequate to those who have limited their communications from the Unseen purely to sermons and teaching purported to come from higher guides. I do not wish to criticize these, for they help many people. I have heard many of them, but personally have found nothing new in them, only a reiteration of material already contained in one or other of the famous books of the great religions. Perhaps it is good for us to have the old truths phrased afresh, and there are no doubt people in the Unseen who are good at expounding them and like to offer such help. Every man has his Guru. My own view is that they are all parts of the whole and should not be seen as unique or isolated forms of revelation.

Thus I feel that to decry messages given at a practical level and in a personal form is to build an unbalanced edifice for reaching the next world—a house without a ground floor. A world where people live and talk in an atmosphere of perpetual sermons is hardly a natural one. We must drop isolated dogma and specialization and develop our awareness of the Other Life as a whole, building carefully, brick by brick, to reach upwards.

I fully realize that there are dangers in this work, but there are dangers in every new form of communication. Your international traveller may be a smuggler and a rogue, or he may be on a mission of good-will. It is our personal moral responsibility whom we link up with or for what we use our vehicle. Aircraft have brought the terrors of aerial warfare, but they have also made it possible for the leaders of nations to meet within a few hours and talk problems over in the event of a serious international crisis. They also carry ordinary men and women to and fro each normal day, helping them to come to know and understand the peoples of other countries. They are, in fact, an essential part of the social pattern of an evolving world community, without which life can never be safely or fully lived in all parts of the globe. This, I believe, is also true of a growing contact and awareness with the new dimensions which, it is now intended, we should contact. For:

> The revelation of the Spirit is imparted to each, to make the best advantage of it. One learns to speak with wisdom, by the power of the Spirit, another to speak with knowledge, with the same Spirit for his rule; one, through the same Spirit, is given faith; another, through the same Spirit, powers of healing; one can perform miracles, one can prophesy, another can test the spirit of the prophets; one can speak in different

tongues, another can interpret the tongues; but all this is the work of one and the same Spirit, who distributes his gifts as he will to each severally.

1

Loss

'Childhood is the kingdom where nobody dies—nobody that matters.'

So wrote the poet Edna St Vincent Millay. I think many of us live in this kingdom, even after we have reached years of maturity. I know we did, and it suddenly crumbled to ashes round us when a policeman knocked at our door one day and said to my father:

'You had a son out on his motor-bike today? Well, he died at the Weeford Crossroads near Lichfield at 1.15.'

What appeared to us then to be the tragic end to a purposeful journey (my brother was going up to Oxford to take his medical finals), a blind blow of fate, was really the beginning of a very important journey for all of us, a quest into the Hereafter. For my brother Ralph it brought an entirely new life in another world, for us a new life in the old one illuminated by knowledge from his.

My parents could not know this when the sudden news precipitated itself literally on to their doorstep. The shock was terrible, especially for my father, who was already in frail health. They, in their turn, were faced with the task of breaking the news to me.

Away in the seclusion of a well-known girls' boarding school I was unaware of events in the outside world. The luxuriance of giant beech trees and verdant lawns in midsummer abundance spread an enshrouding peace. If I had thought of anything to do with my brother during prep on that peaceful summer evening of 4 July, it was only to recall a strange glimpse I had caught of him a few days previously.

I had been ascending the back stairs, which were assigned to pupils and servants. They were uncarpeted and inhospitable. The perpetual smell of brown Windsor soup which permeated the area was one of the things which always struck with a kind of nausea on the first night of term. The front stairs, only just the other side of a dividing wall, were very different with their soothing cream-pile carpets flowing down white stairs in a setting of grey and white leafed wallpaper.

The back stairs were therefore an area through which I normally hurried with hasty footsteps. That day, however, I had felt compelled to stop and gaze out through one of the heavy sash windows, set high up on the staircase. As I paused I saw a dark-coated figure on a motor-bike going up the steep hill outside. Although he had his back to me, the figure was unmistakable. I realized to my surprise that it was my brother. As I stood gazing after his retreating figure, regretful that he had not looked back, I little knew that he was fading out of my life for ever in the earthly sense and that I should never see him 'alive' in the physical sense again.

In spite of this seeming security, however, in the enclosing grounds there had always been in my mind a strange fear. Looking back, in the light of the events that followed, it might be called a premonition. Whenever I heard the telephone ring in the house, I would always feel apprehensive and pray that it did not bring bad news for me.

I recall that I had heard it on that July evening, and that I waited apprehensively, but as nothing came of it immediately I sank back into a false sense of security. I did not realize that it had conveyed to my house mistress the news of my brother's death and the fact that my parents were on their way to break it to me.

It was not till some hours later, when I was summoned to the remote sanctum of the drawing-room where one so rarely went, that I realized something was wrong. There I found my parents sitting on an upright sofa by the fire, their faces transformed with grief: my father with tears pouring down his cheeks, my mother strangely and stonily composed as she told me the tragic news of the loss of one she loved so passionately.

As there was no train back until the morning we stayed overnight in the town in the lodgings which my parents normally took on Speech Day and other times of rejoicing. They were in the long London Road, an untidy stretch with endless streams of noisy traffic. I have always recalled how, as we walked down it wearily, I was suddenly astounded to see through an open french window a nun kneeling in prayer. Why the window should have been open I cannot imagine. That particular convent school, whichI have since passed frequently, is so zealous to preserve its seclusion that it even has frosted glass over all the large downstairs windows where they open on to a balcony. That a nun should pray by one when it was open therefore seems very strange. But perhaps, again, it was all a detail in events that are part of a larger plan.

This glimpse of spiritual peace in our mental agony and chaos had a tremendous impact on me. The fact that someone's life held together, that someone believed in God and was in direct communication with Him, was an enormous reassurance. I have always thought since that the sense of privacy and suspicion of cant in any public expression of religion may perhaps be over-stressed in our sophisticated western world.

Although the rooms of the lodgings seemed very dingy and dark, a fact which we had never noticed in earlier, happier days, our landlady did her very best to comfort us by her warm kindness. So many people were kind, but as we travelled back next day by train I realized the peculiarly isolating effect of grief. People in waiting-rooms and carriages stared at us, immediately noticing something strange in our faces. Then, when they recognized the terrible mask of grief spread over them, they drew back, some because they did not want to become involved, others because they hesitated to intrude.

The home where we had all been so happy as a family seemed transformed on our return. It was covered by a great cloud of grief that enveloped everything like a fog. Ralph's body was brought home from the public mortuary. It was my parents' ardent wish that he should come back to the home he loved so well. It added greatly to our mental agony, however, to see his familiar face lying in marble whiteness and deathly silence in the same drawing-room where he had been the centre of so many jubilant tennis parties or quiet evenings after them, playing the piano in the summer twilight.

The house filled with flowers from the many friends who felt they must show some gesture of sympathy. The air became stifling with the sickly smell of wreaths stacked everywhere. The post-box filled with letters of condolence. My mother was proud to receive so many tributes to her beloved son, but reading them only made her cry the more.

When it was all over and the artificial tempo had relaxed, there came a terrible feeling of emptiness, an awareness that we could not always live up to a show of bravery in the days ahead, for never in all our lives here on earth would he come back to join us. The years of separation seemed to stretch into eternity. It was a terrifying thought.

It hit my mother hardest perhaps. My father, himself a clergyman, had his work in the parish, and this gave him some sense of purpose and urgency, some interest outside the darkness of our present home life.

As an adolescent who had built up an image of romantic heroism and endurance through reading the poems and heroic stories of the First World War, I was able to find some form of escape at times. But even this was undermined by the dark grief of my mother, which seemed to permeate everything.

She spoke much of Ralph, which was perhaps a good thing for her. It meant, however, that everything turned on him, and on what he had said and done in the past in a particular situation, until I, at seventeen looking outward to a new life, began to feel almost jealous. When my mother was not speaking of him her features resolved into an expression of intense grief like a terrible external mask covering her normally radiant face. Any expression of enjoyment or happiness seemed almost cruel, since it cut one off from her.

Searching for a way to break out of this darkness, we discussed the possibility of communicating with Ralph through a medium. My father, unlike many clergymen of the time, was not opposed. Even his own father, also a clergyman, had been interested in the subject in a general sense. Being distantly connected (through a cousin's marriage) with Sir Oliver Lodge, my father had made a point of reading most of his books, and Ralph had himself attended some of the meetings of the Psychic Research Society at Oxford.

My mother had read Sir Oliver Lodge's famous book *Raymond* some years before, but had felt rather put off the subject on account of all the minute details mentioned in the communications. She had then rejected the possibility of communication, saying:

'You don't mean to tell me that on coming back they couldn't find something less trivial than that to speak of.'

It was a matter of personal experience. She was not to know until she lost her own dear one how important these things can be as essential evidence of personal survival. If someone reported dead in a great disaster was found to be alive and had to telephone you from the scene through a telephone operator, speaking on an imperfect field telephone which could only allow the transmission of very limited conversation, how could you establish evidence of identity and the unbelievable fact that they lived except by such means?

But fate had a way of breaking through the barriers we make to frustrate events ordained for a wider purpose than our own personal lives. Ralph's life had not been abruptly terminated on earth only because he had an early vocation for the next world, but also because he was meant to form a direct link, a telephone contact, between this world and the next; a function through which he might help far more people than he could have done on earth, even as a busy doctor.

Our highly sympathetic cousin, Winifred Harthan, had lost her own son at about this time through an accident at school. She lent my mother a book which had greatly helped her. It was *The Earthen Vessel* by Lady Glenconner, the story of her own son 'Bim' (Edward Wyndham Tennant) and his communications with her through Sir Oliver Lodge's medium, Mrs Osborne Leonard. My mother read it with some interest.

She would probably not have done anything further about it, however, had she not had a most arresting experience one night. She awoke from sleep suddenly with a vivid thought in her mind.

'Oh, supposing Ralph is trying to get through to us and we are not responding. It is as if he came home from Oxford and knocked at the door and I did not answer it.'

The realization that she might be shutting him out made her sit down and write at once to the author of the book. Unfortunately her first letter miscarried, for the author was no longer

Lady Glenconner, but after being widowed had made a second marriage with Lord Grey of Fallodon, the British Foreign Secretary at the time of the outbreak of the First World War.

Having had no reply, and discovering she had addressed her letter wrongly, she wrote to Lady Grey and also to a Wesleyan minister who was mentioned in the book, the Rev. Charles Drayton Thomas. To the latter she wrote:

> We have lost our only and darling son on 3 July last. He had left me to return to Oxford two hours before he was killed, full of life and the joy of living. He was run into by a young woman motorist who came out of a side-road. He was terribly injured and died within fifteen minutes. . . . We have a dear daughter of seventeen. . . . If we could get any communication from him it would be of unspeakable comfort. . . . I venture to enclose a few letters out of the three hundred and forty which we have received.

Mr Thomas and Lady Grey both responded immediately. They offered a date for a proxy sitting on my parents' behalf to be taken by Mr Thomas with Sir Oliver Lodge's medium, and my mother accepted at once. Being an experienced psychic researcher, Mr Thomas immediately sent a copy of the correspondence he had received from my mother to Mrs Salter of the Society for Psychical Research in London. This was so that any information he received could be checked to establish any new evidence as authentic and unknown to him when it came through at the sitting.

Meanwhile my mother had begun to pray again, and saying, 'Oh God, if this is right let me go on with it. If it is wrong prevent.'

Mr Thomas was also thinking about the sitting and preparing for it. He recalled that his father, who was in the After Life and helped him a great deal with the work of bringing people through, had said previously, 'In case of wanting to bring something to my special attention it would be advisable to write out a message in a brief form and then read it aloud once or more each morning and evening for two or three days.'

Mr Thomas senior had said that he would certainly become

aware of it then, either by being present when it was strongly in his son's thought, or by noticing that thought when next he visited him. He also invited Ralph to come and ask Mr Thomas's father and sister, who would doubtless be in the room at the time, to tell him how to prepare some evidential messages to send to his parents in the forthcoming sitting.

Perhaps it was this faithful preparation and consideration which made the way so clear. Mr Thomas himself, having fulfilled his duties, had forgotten about his father's advice. Once the sitting had begun and Mrs Osborne Leonard was in a trance, Feda, her control, came through from the Other Life and exclaimed:

> Have you been asked to help a boy? There is one here in a rush to come. He is not a boy who has been ill. His passing was sudden. 'The letter, the letter,' he keeps on saying, as if a letter made you think of him.

Then, obviously having taken into account the instructions given by Mr Thomas senior, Ralph proceeded to reiterate small but telling points in our family life that were quite unknown to Mr Thomas on earth. The letters of condolence my mother had shown him had related purely to his fine character and given no clues to our domestic life. It was significant that the material already known to Mr Thomas, and therefore of no evidential value, was never alluded to. 'He tries to say a name that begins with "B", it sounds like "Ber",' Feda reported.

To us this was very relevant. Mrs Bernard was our pet name for a very close friend, a member of a large family, whom we called by her husband's Christian rather than surname, to distinguish her from many other wives in the family. She was aunt to a girl he was fond of, whose part in this story will be described later, and had been the last of our friends to see Ralph alive. She was returning from Mass in the local taxi just as he passed her house, and the driver noticed him and remarked, 'Why, that was young Mr Plant.'

'Oh Lymer,' Mrs Bernard replied, 'I wish you had told me sooner, I would have asked him in.'

My mother, when recalling the accident, had often said, 'Oh

if only they had stopped him, he would have been delayed and not reached the crossroads at exactly the same moment as the woman driver who killed him.'

This name, therefore, had great significance for us in many ways.

Ralph next told Feda how he made a change in the date of his departure. This was perfectly true, and another source of remorse for my mother. He had been planning to go up to Oxford on Saturday, but an invitation had come for him to a tennis party that day at our Rural Dean's house, and so he had postponed his journey.

Then came the crux of the matter—a further reference to the circumstances of his passing, showing the deep concern he had for his mother's anguish.

> The present [he said]. The present. They will know what I mean. I was so pleased. Tell them it had no connection with my passing. I had wanted it and I do not want them to think that it helped me to pass over.

To emphasize this important matter, he waited, methodically and characteristically, while what had been written down by Mr Thomas was read over. It was so typical of his concern for his mother.

The motor-cycle had been a twenty-first-birthday present from our parents. There had been much discussion before it was bought. My mother had always had a dread of his having one—perhaps a premonition of the disaster it would precipitate. Many alternative gifts had been suggested to him, but Ralph had kept firm to the idea of a motor-bike. So, feeling that his careful nature would make him safer on one than most young men, our parents gave in.

To say he was pleased at having it was so very true. He told my mother that sometimes, when he was riding along a road, he saw people looking at him because he was so happy he was singing to himself.

It was therefore of great comfort to hear this fact, which he reiterated here and on many other occasions, that he was intended to die young anyway. It was all in the plan of things, he said, and however anyone had acted it could not have been different.

He next gave the name of 'C' for a place near where he lived. This was quite correct, for the town where we did all our shopping and had many of our friends was called Cheadle.

He remarked that a little before he passed, his people had been talking about building or erecting something in which they were all interested.

This was perfectly true, as we had been planning to enlarge the tiny vicarage; there had been a great deal of discussion and alterations made to the plans to please the ecclesiastical authorities.

He remarked that he had met 'Har', but could not finish the word. It was only long afterwards that I realized this must have meant his cousin Rob Harthan, since it was his mother who had lent us Lady Grey's book and thus precipitated the whole plan to take up psychic communication.

Ralph also said:

> I am glad that the photographs were taken a short time before so that they have some late ones of me as well as the earlier ones. Mother put one in the right-hand drawer. She may have put more there, but I saw her put one in, and I think she placed it in a sheet of paper. It looked to me as if folded in a clean envelope.

Now this last item was perhaps one of the most interesting of all in the light of subsequent events. We could not at the time place it at all, but the outcome will be told later.

My mother and father were overjoyed by all these messages from the proxy sitting when they were forwarded to us. They arrived on one of those bleak November days, the blackness of which can only be appreciated by those who have spent a winter in the industrial north of England. They came by the second post; my father picked up the letters as he left for the church, where my mother had gone ahead to do the altar flowers. When she had finished these she went out to the churchyard to my brother's grave, where he joined her. It was therefore by more than a strange coincidence that, standing by this earthly symbol of life's termination and decay, the great conviction of survival broke through to them. But let me quote from my mother's letters to Mr Thomas:

> My husband and I are overcome with delight; it is such wonderful evidence. I had gone to our darling's grave that evening and there my husband joined me bringing your letter. And we felt as we have never felt since we lost our darling. I can't tell you the joy it is to feel that we have been in communication with him. My heart is full of gratitude.
>
> How we do bless you for what you sent us. I think it saved me from a bad breakdown. I never felt more utterly despondent than on that afternoon. My husband and I can never forget the feeling of confirmed hope and faith that came over us as we stood by the grave and read your letter.

Though these messages had a profound effect on my parents' lives and outlook, I am well aware that they may mean nothing to outsiders, despite the objective evidence contained in them, since they are linked with personal experience and revelation. I find that the first reaction of many people to any communications of this kind is like my mother's was in the first place: 'Why such trivialities?' This is why I want to tell a story which may help to put things into their true perspective while at the same time giving some facts about the technical difficulties gleaned from my brother over long years of contact.

The story of the personal experience of a friend of mine illustrates the position of psychic communication today as well as one of the reasons why it does not make faster progress.

At the turn of the century, an old friend of mine, Lady Stuart-Menteth, then a motherless little girl of about nine, was sent with her nanny to Bournemouth on the south coast to stay with friends at a house called Madeira House, just by the pier. It is still there today, a solid Victorian edifice surrounded by a smooth green lawn, used as a convalescent home for miners; most people who pass it are quite unaware of the part it has played in history.

The hosts, Mr and Mrs Frost, had two pretty twin daughters who used to sit out on the lawn at 11 o'clock in the morning, as was the wont in those leisurely, opulent days, and sip champagne with a handsome Italian student, another guest in the house.

My friend, who was too young for such social activities, used to look on enviously, but her turn came to play a part when the young man set up in the middle of the lawn a rather odd-looking pole with wires sticking out. Then he went to Poole, some miles away, and spoke so that she could distinctly hear his voice uttering some words if she listened very hard by the pole. Only a few words were audible, and little from them, but the fact that she could hear his voice at all seemed a miracle. The young man said he could make his device far better if only he had some money to perfect it.

When her Papa came to visit her some days later, she therefore communicated the boy's need to him in case dear Papa, who had capital to invest, might be able to help. The matter having been broached, Papa was duly taken out on the lawn and shown the wonderful device pointing towards heaven which had excited his little daughter so much. But, alas, his practical businesslike nature reacted violently against the strange contraption. The few mumbled words it relayed seemed of little importance. To his daughter's disappointment he stormed round the pole indignantly, exclaiming loudly, 'Absolute poppycock, absolute poppycock—I won't lend the young man a penny!'

It was a great pity that he failed to understand the inevitable limitations of this device in its early stages, for the young man's name was Marconi, the pole was one of the first aerials ever erected and he was being privileged to view the first steps in a form of communication that would revolutionize the world.

I often feel that those who dismiss psychic communication at its present immature stage as 'absolute poppycock' are making the same mistake. It is an attitude which is a great stumbling-block to its progress, for it prevents many getting further than one brief imperfect contact. Chiefly I think this attitude is brought about by a complete lack of imagination towards the prevailing conditions.

Marconi, when he went to Newfoundland, could only send back a few halting words to the scientists who awaited his communication at Poldhu in Cornwall, though they were well aware of his plan to communicate and did not question the reality of his effort. He was able to substantiate these words by sending letters by the postal service, which would defeat any sceptic. If you imagine anyone communicating without this background of certainty, then you will realize the appalling difficulties of those who try to convince us of the reality of their presence on the Other Side of life and are so often frustrated in their efforts to get through. They need our positive response and encouragement because they cannot reach us unless we from our side build a bridge across to them.

It is therefore essential for us to take an active part to help those on the Other Side to communicate with us by reaching up to them and talking to them and thinking of them; by doing our part to make the bridge over the gap until, at some future date, it becomes a permanently recognized thing and the dividing veil dissolves.

Our great wish after the proxy sitting was to make contact with Ralph ourselves. We might have had to wait a long time had it not been for the kindness of Sir Oliver Lodge. Mrs Leonard was, of course, a much-sought-after sensitive, and to maintain the good quality of her work she was bound to limit her sittings. Sir Oliver, however, always had a few dates reserved for the use of the recently bereaved who were specially in need of contact.

One of these fell to our lot when another sitter was prevented coming. When we received a wire inviting us to take it there was great excitement. London and the south seemed a long way away from our Midland home, in fact an almost unknown world. But Sir Oliver Lodge's secretary, Miss Nea Walker, thoughtfully followed the wire up with a letter giving us all introductions.

Mr Drayton Thomas and Lady Grey both kindly offered hospitality. Lady Grey's letter was delayed owing to being misdirected, so we accepted Mr Thomas's invitation without question, and it was from his house in Bromley that he kindly drove us over to Mrs Leonard's house for our first sitting with Ralph, and from this visit grew up a life-long friendship.

It was to us quite an adventure and an unprecedented extravagance to journey so far in those days. The Thomases lived in a fine solid house in the flourishing suburb of Bromley, Kent.

It seemed very cosy and cheerful after the bleak north when we arrived on a winter's day. There was an impressive sweep of gravel to the front door, nestling in a wealth of shrubs. At the back of the house the long garden was bordered by a high thick hedge, sheltering it from harsh weather or neighbours and imbuing it with a feeling of quiet and peace. There were beds of roses let into the immaculately kept lawn, still blossoming late into the year.

The house, furnished at the beginning of the century, was a typical Nonconformist home, with everything solid and good in a quiet way, but with no frills or extravagances.

We found Mr Thomas a tall, rosy-cheeked man with a cheerful friendly manner. Though in his late fifties, he bounced about with the alacrity of a schoolboy. He seemed a totally unfrustrated person, pursuing with enormous energy his quest to prove the reality of life after death and bridge the great gap for the comfort of mankind.

Before training for the ministry his father had insisted that he should enter the business world for a year and had put him in a drapery concern. Even in those days there was an interest in psychic research in the family. He and his sister used to work a tumbler with letters, but it was only later, when she died suddenly of appendicitis leaving a husband and a young family, that he took up psychic research as a full-time occupation. The training for the two quite different spheres of life helped to make him the perfect researcher, kindly and forward-looking, but astute and realistic, never accepting a piece of psychic evidence until it seemed logically proved.

Upstairs he had a delightful study looking on to the peaceful back garden. It was lined with shelves filled with his books and meticulous records taken at all the sittings he had attended. I have happy memories of that place; it was here that he would call us to come and hear some choice piece of evidence or knowledge he had recently gleaned, proffering it with professional detachment, but with the conviction of a connoisseur. It was from this room, too, that the first 'telephone message' had gone out to Ralph calling him to the historic sitting when Feda said, 'There is a boy here in a rush to come.'

Mrs Thomas did not have the remarkable exuberance of her

husband, but moved at a more cautious pace, looking after the problems of the household. The foundations of the domestic régime were firmly integrated in two unique maid-servants, Cook and Ellen. Their rosy cheeks and starched aprons shone brightly, as did every inch of the house. They looked exactly as if they had stepped out of Mrs Beeton's cookery book when they sallied forth from the kitchen with expressions of suitable piety to attend family prayers.

With his taste for the best and most reliable in everything, Mr Thomas kept a Rolls-Royce, an open tourer of elegant green which, like the servants, had been a pillar of the household for some time and was even a little antique in appearance. It was very high with deeply scalloped doors which swung open and dangled in the air high above. You had to pull yourself up into the seats rather like a mountaineer gaining footholds on a high ledge, but what a wonderful view there was to be had from the summit.

I especially remember a sightseeing tour we took in it on a very bleak wintry day round Blackheath, which, unlike its name, is a vast green plateau high above the Thames, just behind Greenwich Observatory. The wind felt as if it had come straight from Siberia, and considering Blackheath's geographical position, it may well have done. The curtains of the car did not fit exactly, and let in small pinpointed draughts like jets of cold water from a shower bath, concentrated mostly on the face and neck. Mr Thomas rode buoyant and optimistic in the driving-seat, so warmed with the joy of life that he did not seem to feel the draughts at all. I tried to screw myself up into a corner, but it was impossible to avoid them. Later I developed a terrible sore throat, though it may not have been entirely due to the car, but as much to the strain of being plunged into an entirely new environment full of strange experiences.

It was really extremely bewildering to leave all the familiar landmarks of home. The way and tempo of life in northern England was so different from the sophisticated south, with its illimitable built-up areas merging into the huge city of London. In some ways it was a painful experience, but looking back I realize how it was all a plan by those on the Other Side of life to widen our horizon. At the same time it seemed to enlarge our circle of friends, ready for life in London and the work that was to come. But we could not yet know this.

When Mr Thomas realized what an interesting communication he had had from Ralph, he decided to submit an article about it to the *Methodist Recorder*. He called it 'A voice from the Dead'. It is a tribute to his reputation as a psychic researcher of complete integrity that the article was accepted and published by the official journal of the Methodist Church. In those days psychic matters were not discussed in Church circles as freely as they are today.

As a result he received a letter from a fellow Wesleyan minister called Peel, who had just retired from the West Country and come to live near Bromley. In it Mr Peel asked:

> Does the medical student you mention in your article 'A Voice from the Dead' happen to be Ralph Plant, because he was my son's friend at Oxford? I am interested in psychic research, and should like to come and see you.

Mr Thomas wrote back at once that it was, and explained that by a strange coincidence the Plants were coming to stay with him, so would the Peels come and meet them for tea one day.

When Mr Thomas told us whom he had invited we recalled how we used to pack up strange parcels of bones and send them away to a young man, John Peel, at Bodmin, because he and Ralph shared a skeleton for their medical studies. We had never met him, and when Ralph died he had written a polite little note of condolence. We had not expected to hear from him again, certainly not to see him, since he lived so far away. Probably in the ordinary course of events we should never have done so, but things were to take a different turn.

When Mr Peel arrived, he told us it was a most strange thing how we seemed to be linked for he had heard of us, not only through Mr Thomas, but also by a 'chance' encounter they had had travelling up from Bodmin on the long-distance train. A somewhat talkative lady had got into conversation with them in their compartment; she was not normally on that line, she said, but happened to be returning from a visit to a brother in the West Country. She spoke of how some people had been staying with her because they had come to fetch their daughter from a nearby school when their medical-student son had been killed on a motor-bike going up to Oxford. On inquiry the Peels, to their astonishment, found that the boy was Ralph.

Mr Peel was a most vigorous and intelligent little man—a strange mixture of Victorian toughness and a friendly warmth and interest in life. He sympathized greatly with us, having lost his eldest and very brilliant son, whose promising career had also been cut short when he was killed in the war.

Mrs Peel was a very sweet and charming person, but rather shy, forming a loyal and supporting background to her extrovert partner. John, who was very thin and youthful looking, at that time seemed a quiet, reticent kind of person to me. Being in my teens I did not perceive the great qualities of character and mental brilliance which underlay his quiet manner and which were to blossom later.

We must have carried on a conversation together in spite of my shyness and his reserve, for I recall that, while the older folk were talking, he confided to me that he had just spent his first day at the hospital where he was to work, and that it was a dreadful place.

'It's so big,' he said. 'You can't find your way about. The patients don't know and the staff are too busy to tell you.'

Little did we know then that he was to become one of the most famous doctors there and that his name would go out on news bulletins all over the world while an anxious nation waited for news of the birth of the Royal babies.

I recall that he smiled as he spoke of this difficulty, and I was later to see how this was one of his many valuable qualities—his calm and almost humorous enjoyment of any problem and his power to overcome it. In moments of illness and family crisis he proved a very good friend. No wonder Ralph took such pains from the Other Side to link us.

Perhaps Ralph, in his turn, also tried to do his bit to repay his kindness. Once, another specialist friend (who knows nothing of our psychic communications) happened to remark, 'What an extraordinary intuitive diagnostic your friend Peel is. I took a patient to him the other day who had been messed about with by several doctors who had been unable to find the cause of her illness. But he, without the least difficulty, seemed to grasp at once what was the matter with her.'

Then I recalled how we had asked my brother at one sitting, 'What work do you do over there?'

'I do medical work still,' Ralph had replied, 'for I see further over here than you can on earth. So I walk the hospitals and impress the doctors with the right diagnosis.'

Has Ralph, therefore, unconsciously influenced the work of his friend? It is impossible to say, for one cannot assess the qualities that make a great man.

Next day we set out for our sitting with Mrs Leonard. I do not remember it particularly, but on looking back it all seems a piece with the wonderful and unique rendezvous we had with our friends on the Other Side. They began the minute she had fallen asleep in her chair, after breathing deeply for a short time. Then the shrill voice of Feda, her control, would come through, crying out jubilantly, 'Good morning good morning I come I come!' How many have shared this joy and felt their hearts warm towards this human telephone operator from the other world.

My mother had been lucky in receiving from Miss Nea Walker (among the many helpful letters she wrote), one containing information about what to expect at a Leonard sitting, and how best to respond:

> I enclose the necessary anonymous introduction, which is all you need say to Mrs Leonard—she only wants to know that you are genuine.
>
> If Feda should say that she has seen your boy before, you could just say, 'Yes'. Don't help her out in that direction, just take what comes. And of course don't tell Mrs Leonard normally anything. If the sitting seems good, it is kind to thank her for the comfort, without giving information, afterwards. But never tell her anything. It only spoils later results. With Feda, you have to use common sense and tact; but never give her information which she has not already got. Your best plan is to tell your boy at home of the chance to communicate, the time, the place, and all your little plans. Then

leave him to tell you what he can. Don't set your minds on one particular type of evidence, give him a free hand to bring what he can. It is your chance to listen to him, he can probably hear you pretty well at home; very likely not completely, but not at all badly; so do your talking there, not at Mrs Leonard's. Of course respond when you understand, just to let him know that.

It takes long training [Miss Nea Walker wrote], to learn how to tackle evidence; many people are over-enthusiastic and not careful enough. One has to keep a constant rein on one's imagination, and one's tongue under lock and key. But that very care is what ultimately yields the evidence we all want. The enthusiasts are all kindness itself, but they don't help the subject on. Just because one is never sure what their evidence is really worth.

You ask (in one place) whether your boy finds it now difficult to talk. Because Feda said, 'He tried to say Ber.' It's not that, it's the difficulty of explaining to Feda what he wants, and of conveying his ideas in the form in which they will travel through. Most of the mediumistic work is pictorial, and impressional, and has to be translated into words by the control. He shows Feda things, sometimes he says things, but you have to remember that it's one mind acting on another now, not a tongue and larynx acting automatically in obedience to one's own mind. He is pouring a stream of thought out to the control, and she has to transmit the results. He has to learn how, too. Don't feel that his training here is wasted, etc.—that's not what was meant. We don't know yet how communication is carried on, but it seems to work on the same kind of lines as telepathy, of which we know little yet. Mrs Leonard is only the telephone used to pass the message through. Feda is the sort of medium 'over there', as far as one can make out.

It may surprise some people to know that a 'medium' is also necessary on the Other Side of Life to make a successful link-up, but when thought of in terms of the telephone, it is perfectly understandable and practical. If we want to ring up Australia we must also contact someone in the exchange over there before the call can be put through. In one of our sittings we were told that Mr Drayton Thomas's father was actually running a class over there to train mediums, just the same as we do here. His daughter Mrs Etta and Feda are both mediums in a sense; we were told in a later sitting that this is why communication through Mrs Leonard was so successful.

While the earthly telephone operator, however, is fully equipped with mechanical and objective devices to relay the message, the psychic one is forced to use her mind as her transmitter and may get the message mixed up or influenced by her own thought; this is the reason why so many people with uncomplicated, unacademic, mental processes, such as children and young people, are chosen as 'controls', because they can put through what the communicator really wants to say, not what the controls think on a subject. In a sense this seems an example of 'revealing truth unto babes and sucklings'.

Feda was only thirteen when she passed to the After Life. She was the wife of a relative of Mrs Leonard, who went out to a job in India. She died there when her first baby was born. She seemed to have the vivacity and quick speech of her Indian background and ancestry, coupled with a certain positive determination that she had possibly acquired from contact with the British. This made her an ideal recipient for the material she transmitted, accepting it without academic criticism, yet sticking firmly to her point when the sitters were inclined to dispute her statement. Her psychic perception and foresight were amazing. She constantly gave information entirely outside the sitter's mind and forecast happenings that seemed impossible at the time, though I seldom, if ever, found her to be wrong in her statements.

She had a characteristic language which delighted everyone who came to know her. Many of her terms became household words to us at home. When describing anything that looked difficult or was likely to be impossible to achieve, she would exclaim sympathetically, 'Oh isn't it noo-sense?', which somehow seemed to sweeten the pill. She would often end her sentences with the words, uttered in a rather childish lisp, 'And so so so,' a more decorative and typical sound for the termination of a sentence, than the businesslike sound of 'etcetera, etcetera'.

I never discovered how far she was aware of the humour and inner meaning in her quaint speech when she uttered such phrases as, 'You are one of the sensitive ones, Ruth, had you been linked with the bellies [i.e. the belligerents] you would have been swamped by this war and lost.' In another sitting, recounting the exact number of people in a place, she remarked, 'Oh yes, there were two adults there and two adultresses.'

After all, the mistake is similar to a singer from Holland who once gave a concert in a friend's drawing-room: on finding it difficult to translate the titles of her songs, she exclaimed, 'Oh you must excuse my English you see I am a Dutchess!'

Feda was essentially human and still aware of the details of dress and femininity.

'Did you want some more ribbon, Mrs Alice?' she asked my mother one day. 'When I came to see you, you were saying you wanted some ribbon, some nice ribbon, not a narrow piece.'

My mother remembered that she had remarked to a friend recently that she wanted some black-and-white seri ribbon for a hat. But, of course, not being psychic my mother had no intuition that Feda was in the room at the time.

Feda was most gay in her choice of clothes when she showed herself to people. In later years, when my father passed over and saw her for the first time, she told us, 'Daddy was very surprised at being friends with an Indian girl who wears blue gauze.'

My mother asked what Daddy's first words were on seeing her: Feda replied, 'He said "Good gracious!" '

Now this was just one of those typical little touches that mean so much. It was so characteristic of him, for he constantly used that word in mock alarm in any startling situations.

She appears to have made a real contact with my father when he reached the Other Side of Life in later years, and aptly summed up his views in a very characteristic way when she said, 'Daddy liked people to think of God in a sensible way, instead of being full of silly rules and saying things they did not understand. Daddy really wanted them to do good business for God. But he thought some clergymen awful sticks in the mud.' 'Stick in the mud' was another characteristic phrase which my father often used in fun about people. Therefore, even when being amusing, she was giving evidential material, for in spite of her seemingly frivolous feminine side, Feda was well aware of her real vocation as a mediator from the Other Side.

She explained this to us in a later sitting: 'I am only the instrument. It is always better for me to listen till they [the communicators on the Other Side] give it, better it comes from them than from me.'

She was detached when relaying messages but she was ardent in putting over certain principles and truths she had learnt on the Other Side, which she felt were essential knowledge for the earth. Though she seldom dictated about these matters to the sitters, she was very emphatic about them to Gladys Leonard her medium. She was convinced that if Gladys lived out these principles it would be the best way of spreading the truth on this earth.

There is still much argument over whether a medium's controls are real personalities, entities in their own right, or merely split personalities.

The more I knew Feda over those years, the more I have come to think of her as a person entirely separate from Gladys Leonard. The two differed so completely in tempo of life and personal reactions to situations.

The great things that held them both together were, first, the fundamental principles for which they stood, and secondly, the work they had to do together in helping the bereaved and bringing through new knowledge from the Higher Life for the people in this world.

The idea that Feda was a separate entity was further emphasized by the fact that when, in later years, Mrs Leonard retired from her work, she appeared to change tremendously. The more solid English qualities of her character became more apparent. She had far less quick sparkling humour; her pace, both mental and physical, became more dignified and heavy, although she appeared quite normal in health. One felt that the cessation of these daily contacts with Feda's vitality had taken something fundamental from her. Had it been simply another part of her personality it would have still been present, even though the professional rendezvous through sittings had been given up.

During her working life as a medium, Mrs Leonard responded to Feda's partnership with a shared sense of vocation and disciplined obedience. Thus they created a line of communication which was unique and completely fluent. The progress of sittings was never interrupted by such interrogations as, 'Does that mean anything to you?' or 'Can you place this?'

Ralph once alluded to this kind of approach, after we had been to an unsatisfactory medium, as 'summing up psychometry', a phrase invented by Mr Drayton Thomas.

'That medium you went to,' Ralph said, 'was giving what *she* felt about me and not taking in anything I told her.'

With Feda there was no need to question or hesitate; or to resort to these lesser forms of psychic activity. The sitting just flowed on like a conversation in a family. There was never any triteness about the utterances, for Feda took infinite pains to listen to every detail and relay exactly what *they* wanted to say.

Mrs Leonard was completely devoted to building up the perfect channel, and the thread of her true vocation as a medium was woven right through her life. But, to see this fully, we must go right back to the advent of her life on earth. It was most unusual, and one cannot help wondering if it forged some special link with the After Life.

Mrs Leonard's father seems to have always had a restless nature, and it happened that when Gladys was expected he took his wife for a trip on his yacht. He had to put into port hastily one day, however, the baby's arrival becoming imminent. He hurriedly engaged some furnished rooms, as maternity homes were not so easily available in those days, and sent for a doctor. The strain and anxiety reacted badly on his wife and she became very ill.

The doctor and nurse having arrived, Gladys's father sat downstairs tensely awaiting news and thinking over the situation in which he had involved his wife. For a very long time no communication came from the bedroom, and finally, able to bear it no longer, he rushed upstairs, rapped on the bedroom door and demanded to know how things went with his wife. An impatient reply came back: 'The baby is dead and we are fighting for your wife's life.'

'My baby dead!' he gasped. 'Well at least I can have *my* child to hold,' he said and pushed open the door. He picked up the apparently lifeless form and hastily returned to the downstairs room. He sat by the sitting-room fire, rocking her to and fro, and patting her in his arms in an agony and remorse that his little daughter's life should have been lost in this way.

Then suddenly he heard a loud cry. The baby stirred in his arms: Gladys (or Dodo, as his pet name was for her) awoke to life on this planet.

How far did this flashback to the After Life, when her physical body had already arrived on this earth, make some permanent link to serve as a bridge for her work between the two worlds?

Gladys Leonard was subject to visions from early childhood, and she accepted them with the naturalness of a child. When she looked at the dining-room walls and saw what she called 'The Happy Valley', it seemed as normal as if she was looking out of the window on to the garden of a neighbour's house.

Unfortunately, one day she remarked on these views to her father and asked if he did not feel that they were seeing some particularly beautiful lands that day.

Her extraordinary utterance was received with consternation by the entire family. Everybody feared that some form of illness had beset the child. The doctor was called but no illness was discovered. Then parental discipline took over, and she was told that she must not be a naughty girl and imagine things. So yet another wonderful window on to the Unseen was snapped to, as happened too often with children thus gifted in those days.

When she grew up, however, and began to get independent, she felt strongly drawn to attend a Spiritualist chapel, and it was here that she first realized the reality of survival.

Another personal psychic experience soon after further stimulated her interest. She was away from home with a friend when her mother appeared to her at 2 a.m. looking far more young and happy than when she had left her. When she awoke a telegram awaited her saying her mother had died at 2 a.m.

She developed a great desire to go on the stage, especially to use her voice ultimately in opera. In those days the stage was considered rather a dangerous profession. Her parents agreed to her leaving home only if she went to live with the famous theatrical family the Lupinos, whom they knew. It was their cousin, Lupino Lane, who popularized the famous 'Lambeth Walk'.

In the course of her stage engagements Gladys met several girls who were also interested in investigating communication. They were obviously brought together to establish communication, since it was hardly the place you would expect to find them. Sitting in all sorts of odd places, and often only in the brief times waiting to go on to the stage, they established a definite link with Feda—and came to know her origins and intentions.

Feda's great desire was to entrance Gladys because she felt convinced that she was meant to work as a trance medium. At first Gladys felt considerable prejudice against the idea, and when she got over it there did not seem enough power to enable her to do it.

Then, a strange thing happened. Finding that the ordinary dressing-room at the Palladium in the West End, where she was working, was too crowded for psychic sessions, she and her friends surreptitiously went down to a corner in the large basement area under the theatre where the heating apparatus and so forth was built.

One day during a session they were embarrassed to see the managing director and builder of the theatre, Sir Walter Gibbons, come down there too. Strangely enough, he took little notice of them, but went pacing to and fro with his hands behind his back as if cogitating on some problem of his own.

'Will he never go—will he never go?' the girls said, very surprised he had not ordered them upstairs again peremptorily. But he was not intended to go, for while he was walking up and down two important things were happening. First, the great psychic power which Sir Walter himself possessed was building up for Feda to make use of. And secondly, his presence was creating just that point of interest to take Mrs Leonard's thoughts away from her own problems. How often little things seem to do this and those on the Other Side use the opportunity to pop something into our subconscious. She began to feel very sleepy. Perhaps I could have a doze just to fill in the time, she thought. She did.

When she awoke, she felt she had just been sleeping for many hours, but found her friends gathered excitedly round her. She had been entranced and Feda had given her the first Leonard sitting, providing evidential messages to all the members of the group.

Later on, during the war, Sir Walter, in army uniform and quite unrecognizable to Mrs Leonard, came anonymously as a sitter. During the sitting, however, Feda recognized him and told him of this previous episode and how she had influenced him to come downstairs to the basement of the theatre to give power so that Mrs Leonard could go into trance.

Once she had realized her true vocation she gave up her whole life to this work, always aiming at quality rather than quantity. She never for one moment let herself deviate from the way of life best for her mediumship.

The tempo of the modern medium is so different from Mrs Leonard's. This is perhaps why much that is given at sittings today is mere psychometry, or the medium's own clairvoyance, without any direct contact being made with an individual relative in the Unseen. Mrs Leonard gave up what might have been a successful and crowded social life for the sake of her gift. She loved gaiety and friends, but she knew that going to large gatherings, late nights and even a normal amount of drink, was not good for her sensitive make-up. Large groups of people with all their multiple problems and radiations might sap her psychic power, although she was trained and knew how to safeguard herself. So many vibrations draw too much from a sensitive. She led a happy, active life, but never one which led to rush or crowds, or eating or drinking anything that did not suit her, being most of the time at her home and out of doors a great deal in her beloved garden; she moved at an even tempo that kept her faculties alive and yet uncrowded with nebulous impressions which might prevent those on the Other Side from putting over messages accurately.

Perhaps a picture of her life may be conveyed by a quotation from her book *My Life in Two Worlds*:

> I myself have not found that the development of psychic awareness detracts in any way from so-called normal studies. I am a more successful gardener than I used to be. I am a

much better cook. In many quite ordinary but useful directions I have improved. My health and nerves are under better control and are more to be relied upon than they ever were before I developed what many people think of as an abnormal gift.

2

The nature of the spirit body and problems of communication

When we went for our early sittings to Mrs Leonard, she lived at Kenley, in Surrey. Being so near the metropolis, a mass of small suburban houses flanked the main road that ran past her house and covered the rising ground above.

Garston House, where she lived, was a kind of antique oasis in the midst of it all. It lay in a hollow some way back from the road and sheltered by sloping grass lawns and a garden full of shrubs. It was built on old cellars, which were probably much older than the existing structure.

It was ideally situated, for the low-lying sheltered position protected it not only from the noise and racket of the rushing world outside, but also preserved certain psychic conditions that had built up there in the past.

Mrs Leonard had seen several 'ghosts' there extremely clearly. One had been so materialized on our sphere that he had actually unbolted a door when leaving the house, instead of passing through it in his etheric body, as most apparitions do.

I used to think that when psychics spoke of vibrations and building up psychic power it was illogical and unimportant to our world of reality; the oft-repeated phrase of the ordinary medium—'I want to get a link with the communicator'—seemed to be only a cliché. This was before I had had any personal experience to convince me of the truth of how thoughts connect the two worlds.

We know the air is full of waves; we become aware of this easily today, because the moment we switch on our wireless or TV their effect is revealed to us. But I have become convinced that there are also many other waves of which we as yet know little. Probably of a higher frequency than those so far observed and charted by orthodox science, they connect us with the Other Side of Life. Somehow they are attracted and preserved by previous earth memories down the years, and by any sheltering or enclosing conditions which help them to remain.

One personal experience helped me to understand in a new way why the atmosphere of a house matters. It occurred when we built the house I live in now, on entirely undeveloped land in the middle of a field. Not even the land itself was particularly old, for judging from the poor quality of the soil it was suggested that it had mostly been thrown up from the railway cutting just below when the line was built about eighty years before.

The first night we moved in I was terribly tired, having been moving heavy furniture about and unpacking things till very late. I fell heavily asleep and in the early morning was aware I had left my fatigued body, limp with excessive physical effort, in bed, and had been out on an etheric journey and now was finding it difficult to get back into my body. It was because of the lack of earth memories or thoughts of any kind to surround the house, and I felt almost in a vacuum. I needed these to draw me back like a magnet to earth, to form a ladder I could slide down. I was like an aeroplane looking for a runway to land on, but unable to find one; but eventually I succeeded somehow.

The reverse was true of Garston House; it was full of earth memories over the centuries—one of the reasons which made it so ideal for psychic work. The charming but normal sitting-room, furnished in dark oak with comfortable easy chairs, had become a crucible of knowledge and comfort which was earthly but also coming down from the Other Spheres each day.

Mrs Leonard being a trance medium, the curtains were drawn during sittings to shelter the light from her eyes. The only light in the room was a small electric lamp for the note-taker, and this was poised over her work and shaded from Mrs Leonard's eyes.

We were lucky in our stenographer, Mrs Muriel Hankey, who afterwards became President of the College of Psychic Science and to whose verbatim reports of our many sittings I am indebted for many of the quotations in this book.

Ralph told us during these early sittings of many things connected with his passing and very interesting facts about his new spirit body.

'He wishes to say he did not suffer when he passed,' Feda said. ' "Feared you might imagine I had," he says. "I knew if your mind kept revolving round that thought, it would make an atmosphere difficult for me to get through." He tried to help you get away from that, to clear it out.' Then Feda added, 'He wants to say he felt practically nothing, because the time before he became unconscious was too short to feel much.'

Ralph had more to say about his physical body:

> You know I do not want you to think of my old body. I have this new body which I apparently possessed all the time I was in the old one. It seems very familiar to me.
>
> I know it is the soul's body which lives within the physical body and which survives death. This invisible body is waiting all the time to receive and envelope you when you leave the flesh one. My old physical body has no connection with me now. It would really be more appropriate to think of, stand near and mourn over my old clothes; for they are less of the earth earthy than my old body. Flesh is nothing when once you have left it. The soul has its own body, has it during physical life, and escapes into it from the limitations of the flesh, glad to cast off the limiting earth body. I do not mean that we must regard the physical body as being of no account, because anything God-given must be important till taken from us. The earthly body is important while we are in it but not afterwards. So do not worry about mine.

In our own sittings, as well as the first proxy taken by Mr Drayton Thomas, Ralph took pains to stress again that it was not the bike that caused his death. If it had not been an accident, it would have been some other reason for his passing when he did. I quote some material from the notes about this from our sittings, as it throws some light on the question of how far our passing occurs at its destined time and how far carelessness may even upset this destiny. Ralph said:

> One of the first messages that I ever gave was to say that it wasn't the bike that killed me. You must not blame the present. Now to you that seemed contradictory because you

thought it was the present that killed me. I don't want you to blame it on the poor old bike, or feel responsible for it, and feel if you had not done such and such I should have been safe.

The bike was only a means, an instrument, it was not the cause because I was never careless. I had too much sense of responsibility in such an important matter. I was not absent-minded at the time, I was not off my guard. It was inevitable; I could not have escaped it.

After he passed, the thought came back to him about the time being altered. Had the original time been stuck to, would it have made any difference? No.

There was something inevitable about my passing, and I was meant to go young. God hadn't forgotten me. I was being taken care of, even at that very moment. There was a purpose, and that reconciled me more than anything to having come over here.

It was at one of the proxy sittings that Mr Drayton Thomas asked him the direct question: 'How did you know you were dead, Ralph?'

To this, Ralph replied: 'I did knot now I was dead, I said when I awoke "I am late, again I am late." '

Now, this was just one of those simple little sentences that meant so much to us as evidence through the emphasis on the word 'again'. Ralph had had mumps badly in the spring. My mother was anxious about him after the illness and felt he should rest. So she had let him sleep on one morning. But Ralph had said most emphatically that he must be woken punctually at eight o'clock, or he would never get through his work for his finals.

'It is only mistaken affection to let me sleep on,' he pointed out. 'Otherwise I shall have to work all night when I get back for the term at Oxford.'

Therefore it was so natural that, on awakening on the Other Side, his immediate reaction should be 'Oh, Mummy has let me oversleep again.'

'Then,' he said, 'relatives I had known only from photos came round me and I realized what had happened, and that I must be dead.' This made a link with the message given to us in our own sitting, telling us how it was his maternal grandmother who had greeted him and whose face he knew but he could not say why at first. There was always a photo of her in the sitting-room.

> I make a special effort to help those who come over and are not ready [Ralph continued], because it is a very queer feeling when you first arrive, and you think to yourself 'Where am I? What place is this? Where have I arrived?' You keep on saying this and then you say 'Well it looks the same.' You are aware something is different because you feel lighter and easier, and yet you look at yourself and see you have finger nails and you see even the pores of the skin are just the same.
>
> When I woke up I could see the scratch I had got the day before I passed—it had not faded. Of course those things do fade, but the moment you pass over they are imprinted on the etheric body; even a bad wound you have had for some time but had not thought about would show at first. But an injury which had killed you and which you had not had in life you would not have, because that has not become part of the mind. When you look and see the scratch and everything just the same you say something has happened, but what is it? You feel lighter, you find it easier to move about, you lift your leg and it goes up. It was such a treat to me to think I could go about travelling to see the people and be interested in the things I liked on earth.
>
> Many scientists [Ralph said] think that because our brains are physical brains and are left in the cast-off body, that we have got nothing left to think with. Well of course they have forgotten about the etheric body which has an etheric brain duplicating everything contained in the physical body and brain. That is the body and brain with which people have visited other places and countries at long distances when it has been reported that they have been seen at places far from their home. People can't deny that this has taken place. They did not go in their earth body, they went in their etheric

body and used their etheric brains to find out where they had to go to.

I have got my etheric body now [he continued], and my etheric brain that can think. Now the only reason you can't see me is that my body is etheric and yours is physical, but you must remember that even your physical body is partly etheric. It is only a little thicker than ours but that little thickness makes it hard and difficult for you to see me.

Ralph added:

But of course at night time, when you come over to us in your etheric bodies, which you travel in, in themselves they are the same as ours. They are in the same degree because they are all on the same plane of being and consciousness. Then of course we can see each other and talk to each other.

When you heard I had passed over I knew you would say to yourself—'He can't be inactive. He can't be resting, he must be alive he must be somewhere.' I knew you would say all that and I knew you would try to find me.

When I realized what had happened I knew you would come. I did not know how or where or anything. I was back with you, close to you, before you wrote to Mr Drayton Thomas. I kept impressing you to write to him, to ask him to get a message. I kept saying to you, 'Do, *do* try now, it won't do any harm—try!'

In a later sitting Ralph praised his mother for her courage and perseverance and prayers by which she had brought communication about in the right way.

You know dear [Ralph said], I am becoming quite a centre of attraction here, so many people come round me when they know I communicate. They want to know how I do it, why I do it and if they can do it too.

Most people who come over here have got people who would contact them, but they are not in my position, able to get through and tell their relatives how to do it.

C.D.T.: Yes, but you found it was so surprisingly easy?

RALPH: Yes, it was easy, but you see I hadn't had any feeling that it wouldn't be easy. I simply walked in and did it. It was when I began to think, and have to think, and not be quite so natural about it, you know—at that other place—[the sitting through another medium].

C.D.T.: Oh yes; yes.

RALPH: It was where it struck me first it wasn't easy.

C.D.T.: You felt you weren't so successful then as you would hope to be?

RALPH: I became conscious of the difficulty within—I suppose in your time—five minutes after beginning.

C.D.T.: Ah yes. Did you realize that you weren't getting your thoughts expressed by the medium properly?

RALPH: Didn't realize that first. That wasn't the first thing that struck me.

C.D.T.: What was it then?

RALPH: All I can call it is a tightness. Seemed a tightness and a blank at the same time. I can't explain to you the extraordinary feeling of strain. I felt as if I was using an instrument that was quivering in my grasp.

C.D.T.: Yes; yes. That is very interesting.

RALPH: You see, it didn't feel easy and steady, fitting in with me easily. And then you see, they [the sitters] couldn't help.

C.D.T.: No, they couldn't.

RALPH: Now I think if it had been your sitting you would have simply said something or done something to relieve the strain, but you see, there was nothing done to help. I felt as if I was swimming against the tide.

C.D.T.: Was it that they didn't speak as they might have done, that they stayed quite silent? I forget what really happened.

RALPH: They did nothing, and I struggled through with one or two things that were quite correct, but it was having such an extraordinary effect on the brain that I was using; not my brain.

C.D.T.: Quite; the medium's brain?

RALPH: Yes, that I was making mine.

C.D.T.: As we say, the person was getting upset?

RALPH: Yes, the person was getting upset; afraid I didn't give myself time to think much. It is only now I look back and see what it was like, but I was aware that this instrument, this brain, was getting more and more striving, and yet hopeless. It was like something becoming tense, more and more sensitive, till at last it almost shrank from any impression I tried to make upon it.

C.D.T.: Yes, I understand, it must have been very trying.

RALPH: You know—funny feeling. It affected me and it didn't. Most peculiar feeling. I was aware all the time of the instrument, and sense of swimming against the tide. It didn't hurt me, but there was a certain amount of mental strain about it.

You see, when we come to your side you can't hurt us badly, but you can in a sense, if we are in your condition, hurt us mentally. I have discovered that. You can hurt us mentally.

C.D.T.: I am not quite sure that I understand your meaning. Give anyone 'mental pain'? Discomfort? Disappointment?

RALPH: Yes, discomfort and disappointment.

Anxiety I think would be one of the easiest pains of all to give us, but it would only be whilst we were, as your father calls it, in your conditions.

C.D.T.: Oh, quite. I understand that.

RALPH: While we were in your actual environment. As soon as we get away from you, our natural sense of equilibrium would re-establish itself.

Describing an episode of loss of equilibrium in one sitting, Ralph continued:

On one occasion I suddenly found myself I didn't know where. Suddenly I lost touch with you, mother, father and Feda. I began to feel, 'Oh, what is the matter?' I knew I had been in touch before. I made a plunge forward in my great anxiety to get in touch again. Probably, you know, it wasn't a few seconds in all, but I wildly clutched hold of what I thought were the conditions again, but it was a lesson after; directly I felt that I was forgetting something, I didn't attempt to remember it. . . . Two or three times I was able to remember a thing afterwards when I simply let go of a thing that I couldn't remember previously, when they were not wanting me to remember it here.

He had some interesting comments on the difficulty of carrying thoughts from one level of life to the other:

> I usually get your thoughts very strongly when I am actually with you, but I cannot always carry them back. I take them in at the time, I realize them on my own plane, and when I come back to the earth again I seem to lose them. On my own brain I remember perfectly well—it is in bringing them back here that I lose them. It is a system of filtering in some way, filtering so much of it; we are only on the verge, the very beginning.

I understand so well what Ralph meant by this as a result of an experience I had myself, which was very similar but naturally experienced in reverse, i.e. bringing thoughts back from another plane to this earth, for the filtering appears to be two-way.

To relate the episode in detail would take too long and divert attention from the problem being considered. Suffice it to say, that some years ago I received some advance information on cancer research given me by a doctor who appeared several times to me in dreams. After five years I met a doctor on earth who recognized both the theory and the doctor—a close friend with whom he had worked on research into cell diseases. In a later dream I recall being shown something by him, but as the name of the vital enzyme in it was 'cataleaze' it became mixed up in my mind with the problem of two cats I was worried about.

As I came back to earth and semi-consciousness, I heard the doctor's voice saying:

> You silly ass, I have given you the whole character of cataleaze and you have failed to bring the meaning back with you. Still, just to show that you have been with me, I am going to give you something you can grasp in your present state of consciousness [which I knew instinctively was nearer the earth: you might call it waking consciousness], so that you will know that you have been with me.

He then showed me two deep glass containers. One was filled with a large quantity of stuff, which I learnt later was called media, and a thin layer of stuff on top, called culture. The other container had exactly the opposite proportions. I drew a picture and sent it to the doctor on earth a hundred miles away. He wrote back that these were exact pictures of the proportions in his apparatus at that time. They contained cataleaze and hydrogen peroxide, the materials the dream was about, but, he pointed out, I had not been able to give him anything which was not in his earth consciousness.

I had failed to bring back the vital formula regarding the character of cataleaze from the Other Plane which had been set before me so clearly in the dream, and which must have been so clear in Dr Gordon's mind. What is the filter that separates the two worlds; how does it act and how can we eliminate or reduce it to benefit by vital knowledge such as this which they on the Other Side know of and which we in this physical sphere need so urgently? Even there it seems all a matter of gathering together people for research. One does not know everything in a flash. Ralph once remarked: 'The more people who come over here who know something about communication the faster we shall progress.'

Another time Ralph further discussed the problem of controlling his thoughts at a sitting and gave some interesting facts about the etheric brain:

> You know when I come to a sitting it is often so difficult to remember what I wanted to say, our memories function in bits. One moment I can remember one thing and then next I can't remember what I have said.
>
> I have an idea that the brain of the etheric body [he went on] has to function differently and can only take in or use one lobe at a time. That is why we do stupid things, we often make a noise in your room, tap, etc., when we are trying to do something different. But the great thing is to be able to reach you at all.

At one of our proxy sittings, Mr Drayton Thomas asked him: 'Ralph, have you had the opportunity of studying the bodies round you and the brain? Is what I call the etheric brain a fairly good replica of the earthly physical one?'

RALPH: As far as I can judge at present it is a very good replica.

C.D.T.: Does it do the same kind of work?

RALPH: I think it is a better instrument, one might say a more responsive instrument.

C.D.T.: Granting then for the moment I suppose your etheric brain is the instrument by which you can get in touch with your surroundings there. Have you any power of getting in touch with your surroundings other than your etheric brain?

RALPH: Not that I am aware of; it seems to me that everything appeals to me through the etheric brain.

C.D.T.: You don't feel your soul getting information direct?

RALPH: I am inclined to think, Mr Thomas, that my etheric brain is part of my soul.

C.D.T.: I dare say it is inseparable. Supposing you get a clairvoyant glimpse of something at an infinite distance away, wouldn't that be an action of your soul alone, not working through the brain?

RALPH: I do not think so.

Mr Thomas senior then joined in the conversation:

On the earth plane when our physical brains are asleep and we are incapable of seeing things at a great distance our etheric brain sees them, showing that our etheric brain is independent in a sense you see. I think that Ralph means on our side, on this side, the etheric brain can, in a sense, function; at least it sees at a distance from the etheric body. Do you understand. Ralph's etheric body might be sitting in a chair in his room with his Father but his etheric brain is not doing it all the time; but is capable of a kind of telescopic vision.

Ralph commented:

Yes, that is what I have in mind. You understand the etheric brain is no longer limited by the physical body or brain. It is much freer, it can use the telescope more freely and easily.

'When I am communicating I can see part of you, but not Ruth too,' Ralph said to my mother in a sitting. 'This is when I am waiting or hesitating; but when I am concentrating on Feda, I can't see you at all.'

In another sitting which Mr Drayton Thomas took for us at a later date, he asked Ralph a question that set off an interesting conversation on the problems of the communicator, and why he becomes bewildered.

'You find it rather difficult, this condition of a sitting, Ralph?' asked Mr Drayton Thomas.

'I find it difficult sometimes to know if I am giving the details correctly. I think I have got something to say. I write it down on the atmosphere while I am getting the two facts in relation to it ready, and then very often I forget whether I have given it or not.'

'Ralph, as a medical student with some knowledge of psychology, how do you explain this bewilderment that comes over people when they communicate? You don't feel it in your own sphere I take it. What is the cause of it?'

'I do not think it is something in themselves. I think it is that they are what you might call at sea, as you say on earth.'

'I am wondering why?'

RALPH: It is a physical condition as I understand it, a physical condition. A man on a platform feels all right and speaks all right. The same man with the same qualities goes up in a balloon, on the top of a mountain, in an aeroplane, to a certain altitude where the conditions of the atmosphere affect him mentally. They affect him so that probably he cannot think. An anaesthetic is something analogous in a way in the physical condition and atmosphere of the sitting; what your father calls the power in a sitting affects our consciousness.

C.D.T.: Yes, do you never get any such feeling in your own sphere?

RALPH: Oh dear, no.

C.D.T.: Do you never get such a feeling when you visit your home or your people?

RALPH: The same feeling but a different feeling, it is more a feeling of being limited to a very small area at times. I have been to see my mother sometimes, and some times I have seen her clearly, but not always seen her surroundings.

C.D.T.: Isn't it analogous to our looking at things through a microscope? We see things, but our vision is limited.

RALPH: Very much the same. You can get microscopes and microscopes. You get a poor one and you cannot see as clearly.

C.D.T.: Quite true.

RALPH: We are capable of controlling our own mental conditions to a very great extent. They are not likely to interfere actively. But supposing mother was very distracted by something, concentrating and thinking very emotionally of something, apart from me altogether, connected with another person on the earth. It would not prevent me coming to her, feeling I was with her, helping her, but it might prevent heı feeling me for the time. Unless she switched off from the other person and made herself receptive so that she could feel me, and see me.

C.D.T.: Although this concentration prevented her from seeing you, I suppose it would not prevent you from seeing her.

RALPH: Yes it does interfere. That is not only my own opinion it is the opinion of many others. Our powers of observation are sometimes limited by the mental conditions round you on the earth.

C.D.T.: The more distracted we are and the less attentive to you in your realms the less you can observe us?

RALPH: That is so.

Feda played her part also in trying to contribute some more information to this strange process of communication, about which we knew so little.

Referring to an inquiry we made after a little girl who had passed on, and whose age at passing she had given as older than was correct, Feda explained, 'She was a bright intelligent little girl, and that may be making me feel she was a bit older than she was in reality. You see Ralph was giving me that, not by what he said but by feeling.'

C.D.T.: Perhaps he was just thinking about that and you got it without his intention?

FEDA: Yes, I think so. I think I was getting it when he did not know. With a communicator who is a good one I don't just work away from them. There are times in the sitting when we work together.

C.D.T.: In touch with the same brain?

FEDA: Yes, it is just as if we were controlling the same brain. Mr Thomas does it and Mrs Etta. Only they let Feda speak. I do the talking and they do the language. That is why when Mr Thomas does it I get better words and say things correctly because they put it through me.

C.D.T.: They put it through you? Do you know a word before you hear the medium speak it?

FEDA: When they do it like that I don't always know till I speak it.

C.D.T.: It has to be put on your consciousness at the same time as the medium's mind?

FEDA: I think it is simultaneous. It seems to all come at once like that when they are clever enough to work the brain for me.

Feda praised Ralph for his talents as a good communicator because of his good memory and concentration (characteristics of his on earth). Ralph replied:

> That is what is going to make it easier for you to hear me, when I can pound away through this wall whatever it is. I don't really know quite what it is myself, but I am going to find out and to get through to you.
>
> If only people [i.e. communicators] had better memories, they could help us to sift out in these rather difficult conditions many things that without meaning to we make a muddle of.

This problem of getting things into the medium's brain brings us to the question of putting over names. Sitters are so often disappointed or made suspicious when this obvious means of identification is given inadequately or even incorrectly in communications from the After Life.

Here again we must resort to the simile of the telephone operator. Take my name, for instance. I find that 'Plant' is a particularly difficult one to get through even on the ordinary phone in this earthly sphere. Any stranger having to transmit it invariably gets it as Clark, and when I repeat 'Plant' in exasperation, they reply, 'Oh yes—I've got it—Parkes'. In fact, if I am leaving my name in a message for a friend who knows me by my first name, I often give up the struggle to get my surname through and just say 'Ruth'. The latter is not only an easier sound to hear, but it is a name with which the operator is familiar and so 'rings a bell', to use a colloquial phrase, in the operator's ear and brain.

All this applies as much to the psychic operator, or medium. It accounts for names being left out, or becoming confused in communication, and people have to realize that they cannot give their full name and address as if they were ordering something from a shop. When, for instance, Ralph wanted to link us up with the parents of a friend of his over there, all he could say was, 'My friend's name is Jim, his mother is Betty and they live at Hampstead.' Luckily Mr Thomas provided the link.

In Mrs Leonard's sittings there was a remarkable phenomenon called 'Direct Voice', which served as another form of identification. It was an extraordinary experience to be talking to Feda and suddenly hear Ralph's familiar voice come out of the atmosphere beside us. It was only a few words that he seemed to be able to reproduce in a soft voice, but it was very convincing in spite of its brevity.

His tone was exactly like the one he always used if we were ill and he came into the sick-room to discuss some problem with whoever was in charge, but did not want to disturb the patient.

That this was not just our imagination or wishful thinking was emphasized one day when we were completely startled by the voice of a strange young man breaking in. The contrast was unmistakable. It was Billie, the son of an old friend of ours, who had been a sitter of Mrs Leonard, but who in later years was unable to come, so we took her messages from him.

I don't recall any explanation of this phenomenon being given by Ralph or Feda, but I have myself observed one factor in it which may be of interest. I specially recall noticing it after my grandmother passed over and Ralph was explaining her arrival on the other side.

'Ralph says his grandmother was very surprised to see . . . What did you say Ralph?' Feda asked. Then, out of the atmosphere, came Ralph's voice quite distinctly: 'Trees and houses.'

Feda, though she could hear our voices on earth perfectly and carry on an intelligent conversation with us, seemed quite unable to hear what Ralph said at all at that time. She asked him what he said, and while we waited in silence she listened, as it were, on her own telephone line, inaudible to us, as all her conversations with Ralph were normally, and then transmitted back to us not knowing we had heard it. 'Granny was so surprised to see trees and houses over there.'

It was as if our voices were all on different frequencies as far as she was concerned, like calls transmitted by an ordinary phone operator, and Ralph's frequency to us was somehow not plugged into Feda's switchboard.

3

Phenomena in the home

Ralph spoke in his communications of being with us in the house. This became apparent as time went on and he built up more power. He was determined to make us aware of his presence by various means.

One of the most interesting phenomena he produced was connected with the photos he mentioned in his first sitting with Mr Drayton Thomas and which at the time we were unable to identify.

Many weeks after our first sitting my mother remembered that I had taken a photo of her and Ralph on the tennis court at Easter, only a few weeks before he died. It was the last one ever taken of him. She was therefore very keen to have it. I knew it was on a film which I had taken to school and used for photographing house matches. When a search for it at home proved fruitless we wrote to the house matron about it, but she could only reply that she had packed up all my things to be sent on after me when I was called home suddenly on Ralph's death. If it was not among them it must have been thrown away.

My mother craved terribly for that photo and spent hours looking for it. She remembered a little drawer at the back of her desk, where all smaller 'snaps' of this kind were kept, and she hoped it would turn up there. I used to see her go to it time and time again and pull out the drawer and the other small one below it, knock them upside down on her desk and go through every photo. Then she would put her hands inside the framework and feel all round it in case the paper wallet in which such photos usually came from the developer should be wedged anywhere inside or at the back. But nothing resulted from her intensive searches. Most people would have given it up as useless months before, but somehow my mother felt impelled to continue, as if she had a premonition it would bear fruit one day.

I well remember the final occasion when I was beside her and she went to her desk to begin yet another search. Directly she opened the drawer and before she could lift out any photos, however, she gave a cry of amazement and joy. On the top of the pile lay a wallet of *white paper* as Ralph had described in his first messages. It was lying open, and pulled out of one of the side-pockets gazing at her was the very photo of Ralph she had sought so long.

We were astounded. There seemed to be absolutely no normal explanation. We had no domestic help in the house at the time. My mother did all her own work up till then, as she did for so much of her married life. Few people came to the house at that time. There was no one who could play such a trick on us. My father was a person of far too great an integrity, a keen observer of psychic phenomena. He would never put anything there just to please my mother and mislead us.

The photo could not possibly have fallen from a cranny after my mother's extensive search of the whole framework of the drawer. Every circumstance pointed to the return of the photo being by supernatural means, a case of what is known as 'telekinesis', the moving of things by psychic power. Ralph must have been well aware of the photos since he described them in detail in those first messages, though we could not remember putting them there. Perhaps this awareness enabled him to get hold of them and dematerialize them or hide them away in some strange manner for the months they were missing, and then produce them in this wonderful way. The fact that the wallet was open and the very photo she wanted was pulled out looking at her, pointed to the fact that no casual hand had put it there.

That Ralph was in touch with things in our environment at that time was further fairly clearly emphasized by another interesting episode, which also came to us through a proxy (i.e. a third person when we were not present). It came at a much later date through one of the note-takers who often came with us to the sittings, and who was herself a medium, called Marjorie Rowe. She lived in London and had never visited our house, more than one hundred miles away to the north.

She wrote to us one day that Ralph had been to her and said:

> My mother thinks she has collected up all my belongings now, and either given away or put them away somewhere safe. Acually this is not so. In a box or a bag, the only place at all in the house where she keeps things that are rubbish, you will find two new silk things which I wore round my neck. They are not of course of any special value, I don't mind about them, but I thought she herself might like to know they are there and put them away.

My mother knew where he meant. There was only one such place in the house, for she was most particular about tidying up. She kept, however, a thing called 'the bit drawer'—a long box-like affair at the bottom of a huge old chest of drawers in Ralph's room. Its odd location was, I suppose, a relic from nursery days, because the drawer was full of spare pieces of material used by Nannie and my mother for patching clothes when the chest had stood in the nursery. It was not one which Ralph had ever had occasion to open himself.

For some days my mother did not go to the drawer because she felt that it was so unlikely that anything of his would be there and she would only be disappointed. Imagine her joy when she at last opened it and there, on the top, lay two new silk collars which had somehow escaped from his things. Even if they had dropped down the back of the chest (and as she had not taken every drawer out in search of them, like the photos, this cannot actually be discredited), how did Ralph know they were there when we did not? He kept his collars in the small drawers at the top, so they would have had a long and disfiguring journey had they worked their way down the back of several drawers; yet there they were in perfect condition, as if placed there just ready for my mother to pick up.

I think that Ralph must have been able to come very near to our earth sphere in the familiar surroundings of his own room.

Later he made another contact through Marjorie Rowe, which gave my mother some wonderful evidence of his presence with her in the home and his awareness of her great affection for him. It was after we decided that, owing to her exhaustion and weariness from all she had been through, my mother ought to be extravagant and have some daily help in the house.

On this particular morning, Mrs Ratcliffe, who came to work for us, was busy cleaning at the back of the house when she suddenly called out, 'All right, I am coming,' and came down the corridor to the front of the house where we were. My mother was amazed and hastened to assure her that we did not call her. But she was insistent that someone called the name of Mrs Ratcliffe. So convinced was she that she heard a voice that she became worried.

'I hope it is not Edna, my little girl, come home from school ill,' she said.

'But she would not call you by that name,' my mother remarked.

'No, of course,' she replied, 'but they may have sent someone from the school to tell me she is ill.'

She was so convinced that she had heard her name called by someone that she went out into the road and looked up and down it in case someone who wanted to get in touch with her had not liked to come to the house when she was at work there. But there was no one visible.

My mother busied herself upstairs that morning for a while, but none of us noticed what she was doing. It was only when we received a letter from Marjorie Rowe that the situation was further explained.

My brother had been to Marjorie Rowe and told her that he had been with his mother on that particular morning and that he had seen her take up his pillow and put it back in her own room. Now no one on earth knew but my mother that, ever since his passing, she had taken his pillow and always used it herself. She and my father had recently been away for a short holiday, and during their absence friends had lived in the house to look after the animals. As they had occupied the double bedroom, my mother had taken Ralph's pillow back to his room *pro tem*, and it was during this morning devoted to housework that she had had time and thought to restore it again to her room.

Ralph also said that he had seen his mother take something out of the chest of drawers with the blades and rings on it. He could see it lying on her hand. She thought of giving it away, but after a time she put it back.

Ralph added that she must not mind giving it away, he would be quite happy about this.

This message was perfectly accurate. My mother told us she had taken Ralph's pocket-knife out of his drawer. It had certain additional gadgets to it as well as the blades, just as he described. She thought of giving it to my father, but somehow she could not bring herself to part with it even to him, so she put it back again. No one else knew she had done this at all.

The fact that Mrs Ratcliffe heard someone, apparently invisible, calling her name at the time, seems to point further to the fact that Ralph really was there and that he was able to make himself heard clairvoyantly by Mrs Ratcliffe besides observing my mother's actions.

He was not always so successful, alas, especially with mother, who would have been so overwhelmed with joy to hear his voice. But perhaps her very emotion and tension blocked the lines. In one sitting he remarked, 'You were reminded of me by something. You felt depressed and I caught your thought and stood beside you. "I am here! I am here!" I was shouting but alas you could not hear me.'

It was my father who, although he was not known to have any special psychic power, was the one on whom Ralph was able to impress his presence most vividly on one memorable occasion. Possibly the manifestation was helped by the fact that my father was at the time in a place with a very ancient and strange background.

It happened one night when he was worried about the small number of boys in the church choir. So he set off to a lonely house the other side of a wood by the Vicarage, to see if one of two brothers living there would join.

The wood he had to walk through was called St Thomas's Trees. It was perhaps better described by that name than by the word 'wood'. It consisted of a collection of giant beech trees standing very tall and completely bare of undergrowth over an area of exposed hill-top.

The place was full of historic links. The name originated from the fact that, in pre-Reformation days, the land had belonged to St Thomas's Abbey at Stafford, about twenty miles away. On the crown of the hill, from which there was a remarkable expanse of view, there appeared to have been some form of ancient fortification. At one time some excavating had been done there, and Roman coins found. These fortifications probably had some connection with the ancient tower of our village church in the valley below. It was a very rare octagonal (eight-sided) type, and was said to have been originally a watch and defence tower, probably in pre-Christian days.

The land, with all this ancient history attached to it, was therefore particularly full of vibrations of power, which may have helped to make any psychic phenomena possible. It was as father was returning home that he felt a presence beside him. It was a winter night, and darkness had come down as he left the cottage. There was a strong wind blowing, and as he battled through it he felt someone come up beside him. So natural did it seem that he thought one of the boys had followed him from the house to say something further. As he was deaf he knew he might not have heard them call after him.

He stopped and turned round to find out what the person wanted. To his surprise there was no one to be *seen*, but still he felt certain that there was someone there. Then he realized with joy that it was Ralph who stood beside him, and who after that accompanied him for some way.

Speaking of this episode afterwards at a Leonard sitting, Ralph said:

> That evening when I came to Daddy it was just as if I swooped through the wood and met him. I turned and walked close at his side, keeping the sense of my presence as long as I could for him. It helped him as much as anything since my passing, for it was his soul that knew I was there. He felt grateful and so did I. It kept him going.

How far these exterior conditions can contribute to a manifestation like this, taking place in the open air, was discussed in some interesting comments Feda made on the appearance of Walter, the husband of a friend of ours. He was the father of Billie, whom I have already mentioned as he spoke in the direct voice suddenly at one of our sittings.

Billie's father had been Governor of Malta, dying there during his term of office. He was a very fine man, beloved not only by the men who followed him as a general, but by the civilian population. It was not surprising, therefore, that there should be authentic accounts of his appearing to the fishermen on the sea-shore after he passed.

In answer to a direct question I was asked to put by his widow, asking whether he was aware that the fishermen had seen him, Feda replied:

> Yes, that is right, we know all about it. It is quite true, and Walter has been helping the fishermen. He is sorry for them and has been helping to improve their conditions too. Tell her he will be seen again, in the right conditions.

Feda went on:

> When people see in this objective way, it is not clairvoyance; it is objective. It depends on conditions. When you get merely our impressions, you can get these at any time, day or night, hot or cold. The other, however, is like building something up, a kind of half and half process, verging on the edge of both worlds. It is both. The shell of the etheric world slipped over our world, as it were.
>
> Ralph says they need a special condition, a certain steadiness in the atmosphere, it might be a mistiness, but it is dryness usually. Thoughts having been sent out in a kind of general way beforehand you see, all that may help to build up, and enable something to just come up from the etheric stage sufficiently into the physical to be visible. It may only be just for a little while, for a few seconds. Ralph says it is very much similar to a sunset, you go and call somebody and it has changed before you reach the window. Well it is rather like this with these objective visions.

Ralph did succeed in making himself visible to Mrs Leonard, aided no doubt by her great psychic power and the magnetized conditions prevailing at Garston House. It was on 11 November one year when my parents had booked a sitting but had to cancel it because my father was ill. Mrs Leonard was informed, but we forgot to tell Ralph. So having previously caught our thought that we were coming, he turned up at the time arranged.

When we did not appear he got impatient to attract Mrs Leonard's attention and rapped several times on the silver tray in her sitting-room. She heard it, but did not know who was doing it.

As this did not work, he stood on the stairs as she went up to wash her hands, and she noticed him at last. But seeing a young man standing there in a brownish suit, she jumped to the conclusion it was some soldier who was trying to get through as it was Armistice Day. She was puzzled as she did not know any soldier who was likely to do so just then. Ralph was wearing a brown suit almost khaki in colour the day he died, so that was how the confusion arose.

This lack of recognition on Mrs Leonard's part and the fact that she imagined it was a soldier is further evidence of the reality of the appearance. He was not in Mrs Leonard's mind.

When our postponed sitting was held, Ralph alluded to this episode and said:

> I think Gladys saw me on the stairs. I tried to make her do so and I followed her into the place where she was washing her hands. I followed her to the bathroom and made her feel me there because of the running water that was present. It seemed funny [he went on]. I have come to the conclusion that where there is water there is psychic power. People would laugh if you said that Ralph finds bathrooms easy, but it is true. It is where there is water. Jim [alluding to his friend in the spirit] always mentions things in the bathroom to his mother, but he does not know why I do; it is the presence of water and the fact that water is kept moving there. Stagnant water would not have the same effect, it would be lifeless and unpsychic.

I think that this emphasis on the power of moving water is very interesting in view of the appearance of our friend on the sea-shore at Malta and the clear vision which it seems to have been possible to build up there. We find in the Bible many instances of Christ appearing by and on water, and the great miracle of Lourdes took place by a running stream.

As regards the actual physical knocks that Ralph had made, he made an interesting reference with regard to the tray.

'I knocked on the tray because we have one like it at home,' he said. 'So I felt there is something I know. It is slightly different in pattern, the rim is different.'

This, we found, was absolutely correct when we came to compare Mrs Leonard's with our own. It was an oval one like ours, but the edge had a deep rim round it while ours merely sloped up a little. It had been presented to my grandfather by his friends and parishioners after fifty years spent as the much-loved vicar of one parish, and it was a rather cherished family possession which Ralph had known from childhood.

Ralph alluded to another knock he had made, apparently in Mrs Leonard's house, but which had not been identified by her.

'Mrs Leonard wonders,' he went on, 'why there are knocks on Fridays. Well that is the day Mr Drayton Thomas comes for his regular sittings. So if anyone hears me knock they will know I am wondering if Mr Thomas is coming for his sitting that Friday or not. If he is not, please ask Mrs Leonard to tell me. Then I shall know it is no good waiting.'

This seems to stress the importance of telling our friends in the Other World what we are doing beforehand, and of calling them if we want to talk to them. Since they do not live in the time sphere, they cannot always hear exactly what we are planning or altering.

Ralph also made knocks for us in our own home. He began by knocking on the furniture, then, when our minds started trying to puzzle this out and entertaining a slight doubt as to their time origin (perhaps wood might be subject to noise due to climatic changes), he suddenly switched to knocking on the old brass bowls on the top of my father's court cupboard.

My mother used to speak to Ralph when he did these knocks to encourage him, and I think the response helped him. In one sitting he spoke to us of the need of complete naturalness when receiving communications.

'Be quiet,' he said, 'but don't be too quiet, for if you are repressed you repress the power. Be perfectly natural.'

Some people may feel that knocks are a foolish form of phenomena coming from an intelligent young medical student, but I hope these episodes will have shown that they have their purpose, just as the buzzer does on an intercom telephone: someone in the house is wanting to speak to you or at least to demonstrate that they are there.

Sometimes it may represent an urgent call: a reason for deploring the way they are labelled 'poltergeist phenomena' and regarded with curiosity, but with no attempt being made to contact the communicator. Where there are constant hauntings, for instance, it may be that the noise is equivalent to dialling 999 for an ambulance. Someone who has been tied to a place for perhaps hundreds of earthly years is hoping for a spiritual vehicle to take them away, and they should not be disregarded.

4

Advice and help from the Other Side

Later the knocks and similar phenomena became far less frequent and wider interests took our attention. As Ralph explained, now that we were in a happier state of mind about him and about life in general we could appreciate these.

'Don't worry,' he said. 'You are not shutting me out of your life; you get my thoughts. I want you to do as much as you can while here. There is so much to be done and I am in it all. It is selfish to think at the expense of doing.'

> You must learn not to premeditate; take one patch at a time, and you will be given the understanding you need, and told what to say.
>
> Discard what thoughts are wrong as soon as you can decide, because puzzling over them blunts the edge of intuition. If you have to alter something, don't do it with a sense of 'Oh, how can we do this?' because we can help you to do it; it is only your thoughts that make a barrier.

Once, when we had encountered almost insuperable difficulties in a specific scheme to raise money for a motor chair for a crippled friend, Jimmie, and our appeal to the only available charity of those days had been turned down, Ralph said:

> Don't say you will rely on so-and-so specially. You might by that close yourself to some other channel that would otherwise be open to you. Knock on all the doors and we will open the right ones, but you have to knock on them yourselves. If we did the knocking we should be taking away your initiative.

In spite of opposition and indifference, because Jimmie had a slowly progressive form of paralysis we did achieve our goal and get him the chair in which he spent fifteen very happy years.

'It is not achievement that really matters on earth, but what we have really learnt,' Ralph remarked, stressing this so much that it had to be underlined in the notes. 'This is very true of H.,' he went on, mentioning a particular friend we were helping with problems just then. 'He is too impatient to see results. When a door opens and he sees nothing happening at once, he thinks there is nothing coming through it and he slams it, just when things would have worked out to help him.'

I feel myself that what Ralph says here is most important for us on earth to remember, for it shows how people may, so to speak, get out of step with the intended rhythm of their lives and the projects they are working on, and by anxiety and impatience increase rather than decrease their problems.

'I am not always allowed to tell you when you are wrong and to put you right over such matters,' Ralph said. 'You must study them and come to your own conclusions, even if it means taking a certain amount of trouble. If you do not do this when you come over here you won't have gained the ground that will enable us to do things together. By helping you to help other people I am helping myself,' he went on. 'We are never allowed to interfere with free will,' he added. 'We can only influence and suggest.'

This is an important point as so many people are strongly opposed to the idea of communication because they feel it means dictatorship from the Other Side. Yet, on this earth, they will quite naturally accept advice from their friends over their problems and feel that this is a valuable relationship and a sensible co-operation. They cannot see that there is no difference when the friend has passed into the spirit, except that they have an extended knowledge and wisdom to offer. The dangers of domination are purely a matter of personal relationships between individuals, and may occur here or Hereafter. In either case they should be recognized and dealt with.

The great thing is to remain in a positive and calm state of mind ready to receive the impressions that *really* come from the Other Side, not get excited and rush off at the dictates of what is really our own subconscious. We must wait for our instructions and for events to work out in their proper sequence, and not on any account force their progress.

Speaking about this during another sitting, Ralph remarked:

> Things have come to you in lots of unexpected and peculiar ways. I think the old souls get them that way because their guides have been with them so long the oversouls don't expect them to want a good deal of explanation or leading up to things. They expect them to be prepared because of their past experiences.
>
> If you are not biased by other people [he went on], you are ready to perceive them. When you have gone wrong sometimes is when you have told someone else. I have noticed that again and again. I do not feel that you see this as so important. As soon as things begin to shape and unfold themselves and you see they are doing so just be ready to take things in both hands.
>
> If it is the right thing [Ralph continued], we can always overcome the difficulty. Do you know what absolutely knocks our plans for six is when people lose heart a little and they say to themselves, 'I do not think the Guides or the people over there are going to be able to do this; it is too difficult for them.' Then it is just as if you cut a cord between you and ourselves when we are trying to achieve something. It is an invisible but a definite something that is built. It is as important as a web that a spider lets down for what he wants to do on the ground or at lower level, and when it is suddenly snapped the whole operations break down.

In one sitting I specifically asked my brother about healing. There is a note with the sitting which says that I had felt an impression while in the bathroom (another example of the power of water) that he wanted me to know something about it. I had also followed Mr Drayton Thomas's method and had written a letter to Ralph asking him for information.

He began by speaking in a general way about helping people, making the interesting statement that he was now working out part of the early progress he had missed on earth, so it was not a drawback having gone early.

It can be a drawback for us when people on earth worry us by saying 'Why don't you do this, or why don't you do that for someone.' People don't realize that we cannot help to order. [Here I have made a note that the Direct Voice was particularly strong, as if to emphasize this statement.] We have to help them as we can and when we can. That is when the right way opens.

I am not only working through you to help other people, but I am helping myself [Ralph went on]. Your condition suits me in a wonderful way and Mother has helped a great deal since coming over. When on earth I should hardly have thought this possible.

Your mother [observed Feda], was so very fond of Ralph she rather divided you. [This was quite true.] But now she acts as a link, and he really *is* working through you. For some months he has been doing this and impressing you to because you are living in a most important and dangerous chapter of the world's history, which we, and Mr Thomas's father have been telling you about for years, and we must be armed with the spirit of knowledge. So much that was thought important in the past has been blown right away, and even the experts don't know it is very much guess-work. Because of this it is so important to gain in spiritual knowledge. A certain amount can be done by the person who does not know anything about this, but the result is not so good as it might be.

You yourself have healing power, but you are not meant to take it up yet as actual healing. You are a co-ordinator of people, spreading and directing it to people. You have rock-bottom truth; that does not mean you cannot make mistakes, but you can carry an unusual amount of truth with you. Others do it, too. Gladys, for instance. What you and she do is more consistent. Others think they are doing it, but they undo the good they are doing. We don't want you to come over for some time; even the bedridden ones are of use. You are laying the foundation stones for the future. You will know this and have great satisfaction when you come over here.

The observation about the bedridden ones being of use, which I have only recently discovered, is interesting, since Gladys

Leonard was confined to bed for a year or two before she passed. This would seem to be an enjoinder for the future and to give meaning to her forced inactivity, which we all so bemoaned. I wish I had rediscovered it before.

Ralph then made the interesting observation:

> You are doing valuable work not only for us but for those who stand behind us. You don't recall you know these others but you do. [Presumably this referred to some Guides who were specially helping in this work.] Whenever you need this Divine Essence draw it in thinking to yourself 'I am drawing in life'. If you have a pain in your heart or your finger direct it there. If it is a general condition that is disturbing you, think of it giving strength. Think of hope, not negative things, breathe in courage and say to yourself, 'If I make a mistake doing this when I think I am doing good then I shall be helped.' Healing is the most important thing, but it is so simple. The Divine Source of all life, and you must know the way to conduct it to people. All who live by God's Laws are allowed to use its power. Others who are not living by these are not 100 per cent successful. They want to heal but they are not consistent. At the back of this single operation is power, healing, life essence, call it what you will. If a baby is born and cut off from air it dies. The same thing is true of a soul cut off from divine power.

I then asked if patients and healers should be classified into groups like blood donors.

> Well they could be [Feda replied], but they need not be. While people are on earth prejudices do occur. If a patient comes merely saying, 'I am going to see if you can help me,' and has not got the patience, he can come from any group, but the healing will fail. Or if the healer is failing to co-ordinate his life, then there may possibly be no healing.
>
> So we must go back to Jesus, the greatest of all healers. He never failed, over death or disease, or mental trouble, because he was working in accordance with the real source and living according to that source.

Here I asked about the healing of unbelievers.

> There is also the Karmic element that must be taken into consideration. The patient may need a Karmic lesson so that he cannot make the illness the reason for failure. It is to give him a chance; it is up to him whether he takes it or not. There is free will, of course, for we may suggest but we are never allowed to coerce. So you see some curious cases of healing of people who don't seem likely.

I shall limit the section on healing to this, because I feel that it is a vast and important subject that really merits a whole book to itself. I have learnt much since regarding this subject through sources outside our direct psychic communications (though it has been information approved and even sent by those on the Other Side), but simply a different source working into the pattern of destiny. So later, when the pattern is further connected, I will write of it further.

5

We make new friends

As time went on, it became more apparent that Ralph was steadily working out new contacts and wider horizons for us, as he would have done had he been on earth. Looking back, I realize that it was all part of a plan to prepare us for future work beyond the environment in which we were so deeply rooted. This speeding up of events often seems to happen when people link up with those on the Other Side of Life, and it shows why so many previously frustrated people find that things change for the better once they forge the line of communication.

At our sittings Ralph constantly spoke of Jim, his friend in the After Life whose parents he would like us to meet on earth. Ralph stressed that certain details of Jim's passing had been very like his own. He said that he and Jim had both decided that it would be nice for their parents to know each other. Finding them was rather more complicated as Ralph could not get Jim's surname or address through to the earthly sphere. As a clue for how the problem could be solved, however, he said that Jim's mother's name was Betty, they lived in Hampstead and Ian's mother would know them. We did not know who Ian's mother was either at that time, but we inquired about her from Mr Drayton Thomas, who told us.

Ian's mother was a well-known sitter of Gladys Leonard's—a titled lady, who communicated with her own son. He suggested we wrote to her. She replied at once saying of course she knew Jim, her own son was also a friend of his over there. She had already met his parents. Giving us their name and address, she encouraged us to write to them.

Mrs Gilmour, Jim's mother, was the founder and head of the most famous firm of Court dressmakers in those days. She made all the Queen's clothes and most of those for leading actresses.

My mother felt very shy about writing to her and saying, 'Our sons have met in the spirit world and suggest we meet you.' But Ralph had said she must, so she composed a letter and sent it off.

A most warm reply came back in answer. *Of course* they knew who my mother was! Jim had often spoken of her and had been with Ralph to visit our home. Would we come and visit theirs, therefore, and stay with them next time we came to town?

We accepted this invitation to fit in with our next visit to London for a Leonard sitting. No wonder Ralph wanted to link us up with them. How wisely he always planned our new friends. The acceptance of this invitation opened up for us a whole new world.

We arranged to meet Jim's father at Paddington Station arrival platform, as we had been seeing some 'quack' nearby whom we hoped might help my father in his very frail health. My mother insisted that he should stay in the waiting-room for fear he caught cold. So only she and I went out to look for Major Gilmour, our host, whom we had never seen before. In spite of the fact that there was no parson in a dog collar to help him pick us out in the crowd, as he had expected, he came straight up to my mother and said, 'You must be Mrs Plant. I should have known you anywhere from my boy's description of you.'

We duly collected my father and drove in what seemed then to us to be a fabulously grand chauffeur-driven car to their home just off Avenue Road. We turned into a leafy side-road, and stopped outside a low house of a very individual style which went by the rather unsophisticated name of The Cottage. It was a very large edition of any houses we had known by this name at home. There were rotund bow windows at various angles. Perhaps some resemblance to a cottage might have been perceived in its chubby lines.

There was a porch on to the street, with a wrought-iron gate across it. The inner door was made of opaque glass, also set in a decorative iron frame. I had seldom seen such an entrance before. It struck me as very beautiful. The chauffeur pressed the bell when we arrived, and as I stood gazing in wonder at the door, it slid back as if by magic, though actually manipulated by an attentive manservant just inside who was waiting to usher us into what seemed a veritable fairy palace.

The hall was chiefly white marble, as far as I can recall, with some fine Persian rugs and small select pieces of furniture and statuary that gave it a feeling of cool artistry blended with cosiness.

Just inside the door stood Mrs Gilmour, who, to our relief, was not fabulously well dressed. She was clad in a very plain, rather old black dress, though it was ornamented with some very fine jewellery. She took little interest in her *own* clothes, we found later, being too taken up with other people's. The plainness of her garb only helped to offset her fresh colouring and radiant smile of welcome. Without hesitation, she threw her arms round my mother's neck, kissed her, and then turning to her husband said joyously, 'Why Shawmus, we should have known her anywhere, shouldn't we, from Jim's description of her?' We felt at once Ralph had brought us a permanent friend.

From the hall, having given our coats to the attentive manservant, we passed into the lounge, where there were deep-cushioned Knowle sofas and large chairs upholstered in rose pink damask. There was a side-table laden with caviare and the 'White Ladies' popular in those early days of the cocktail. It was an environment entirely different from our normal social life at the Vicarage lounge, with its 'Varsity' basket chairs upholstered in shadow tissue and a tea pot and fruit cake on the oak table.

The cocktails were so potent that they had a rapid effect on my mother's unsophisticated system. She had to confess later that after only one she had been rendered quite incapable of going out to post a letter she had in her pocket.

The lounge led into a music room, the most beautiful room in the house. This was understandable as it was built for Sidney Jones, the famous composer of light operas. It was a long room hung with family portraits rather like a picture gallery, but it culminated in a huge bow window, a kind of Edwardian adaptation of a piece of the Victorian conservatory. The parquet floor was replaced by a black-and-white mosaic floor with a circle of cool ferns and plants round the window. In the centre was a white marble fountain with a reflective figure gazing down at the softly splashing water—the very embodiment of contemplation and leisure.

The large glass doors opened out on to a walled garden enclosed by a high wall of mellowed brick covered with creepers. The air was warm and filled with mingled scents from the flowers in the various beds dotted over the lawn and in the borders round the wall.

Only occasionally was the peace disturbed by the gentle swish of motor-car wheels or the clip-clop of horses' hooves as vehicles passed at a leisurely pace along the quiet road.

On an oval piece of crazy paving just outside the music room stood an exquisite piece of bronze statuary—an upright figure leaning forward a little in deep contemplation, while behind him stood two others, leaning over his shoulders with their faces close to each ear. Underneath the statue were written the words: 'Two voices whisper in the garden, the one to work and the other to play.'

How exactly this reflected the situation. How often I struggled with early literary efforts out there, spurred on by the famous stage personalities I was meeting, and other fresh experiences, yet longing to sink into glorious relaxation and the scented delights of this haven after the exhaustion of the great metropolis and the social whirl.

I little knew then that it was the incredible spectre of war which would eventually disturb the even tempo of our friends the Gilmours' life here, and drive them out of London where, so drastically uprooted, they soon became ill and passed to the After Life.

We were not, however, to see these shadows over the future as we entered into the joys of what was an entirely new life which Ralph intended us to experience. The daily programme was certainly very different at The Cottage from what it was at the Vicarage.

Soon after 8 a.m. an immaculate maid appeared in our room, and drew the flowered chintz curtains back from the large bow window looking on to the garden. Then she brought to each bedside a tray laden with every kind of food one could need for breakfast, served in shining white china patterned with roses, with hot-plates and sparkling silver.

Still a little bewildered and unbelieving, we sat propped up by square-shaped pillows of softest down, so different from the long more lumpy ones at home, and blinked at the trays for a while before beginning to deal with them.

There was no need to get up and rush for the bath while it was free, because everyone here had their own bathroom. There was no cause for hurry over the breakfast either, because nothing happened before 10.30.

The Gilmours put a tremendous lot of work into their business when they were there, but they never got to it much before 11 o'clock. That was something that seemed very strange to me then, knowing only the workers in industry and on the farms at home, who always rose at the crack of dawn.

If we were ready by 10.30, we could get a lift down in the car to the glamorous West End, where we might feast our eyes on clothes which, being then in my late teens, I was beginning to find particularly exciting. My mother, too, since she got into touch with Ralph, had given up wearing black at last and enjoyed having new things. When we had explored the shops we were invited to go and meet Mrs Gilmour at her business, and she always took us out to lunch to some exciting new place. I recall how we consumed hot *hors d'oeuvre* and green beer in a new restaurant patronized by the Duke of Windsor (then the Prince of Wales), and ate amazing curries served in the luscious setting of a famous Indian restaurant.

Sitting on a French-style couch in the large central salon at her showroom, waiting for our hostess, we would watch the interesting procession of clients who came and went to the fitting boxes. I can still recall the Vanbrugh sisters, sweeping across that carpeted floor, one of them wearing a particularly elegant long cape and glancing around with a delicious sparkle in her violet eyes.

All the clothes which clients bought there were made to measure, either from individual models designed by Mrs Gilmour herself or from models from Paris dress shows. These frocks were simply shop-soiled by models slipping them on and off to show customers. Mrs Gilmour, to my amazement, insisted on giving several to me. I felt like Cinderella being clothed by a wave from the magic wand of a fairy godmother. To step from the simple garments purchased by a limited clerical income at our local shops into these famous and fabulous models from Paris was quite staggering.

I am still, after all these years, wearing one dress she gave me —an exquisite model by Molyneux, made of black ring velvet, scattered with sparkling *diamanté* set into it by jewellers. It has never worn out, and being effective in its plain style it seldom looks out of date either.

For my coming-out dress she gave me a dress of delicate pink faille, with a blue bow at the waist. The skirt was edged with silk net, which fell in uneven points like flower petals below. This model had been chosen by Marie Tempest for *The First Mrs Fraser*, in which she played the part of a wife who, having divorced her husband, got on friendly terms with her successor. It was a play which made a great hit in those days, when divorce was seldom spoken of frankly and jealousy and separation between two such wives was taken for granted.

Mrs Gilmour took us to see Marie Tempest at her home in Avenue Road. She was then acting in *The Vinegar Tree*, and I remember we were interested to discover the fact that one actually grew in her garden. I can see her still, standing under it, very crisp and piquante and rather *Parisienne*. We thought she was very sporting, I remember, because she remarked to my mother, who already had white hair, 'Why, I was acting when you were in your cradle!'

The most memorable personality whom I met among Mrs Gilmour's stage friends was, however, Mrs Patrick Campbell. We first saw her in *The Matriarch*, a part which gave her powerful personality much scope. She was made up terrifically heavily, especially about the mouth.

She came back to supper with us at the Cottage after the show with all her make-up still in place, merely exchanging her vast Jewish robes for a somewhat flamboyant dress of printed tulle. It had huge flowers—chrysanthemums, I think—in shades of yellow, running rampant over a background of darkish brown. This whole ensemble was topped by the odd addition of a large picture hat of cream crinoline straw (popular in those days) trimmed with dark velvet ribbon, built up in a cluster of bows. When she arrived she was wearing the bows at the front, but when she departed she was wearing them at the back. I have never been able to decide on which occasion she had it on the right way round. Perhaps she did not know herself.

This small idiosyncrasy in her ensemble did not seem to matter to one whose personality was so strong. She would probably have made the same impact clad only in sackcloth.

The supper awaiting us was not especially glamorous, as far as I can remember. The servants had long ago gone off duty, but they had laid a cold side-table with beer and sandwiches. These our guest consumed with great avidity.

I remember she talked very forcefully in a deep voice, and seemed to fling her ideas out very rapidly and rather erratically directly at one. She would turn and express to you a very definite opinion on something with which you were quite likely to be in complete disagreement, but before you could reply she would look at you firmly and say, 'Yes, my dear, I quite agree with you, you are absolutely right,' making the recipient speechless by surprise through the rapidity of this manoeuvre. Then she would take advantage of the delayed action to sweep the tide of conversation into an entirely new strain, leaving no appropriate opportunity for the matter to be reopened. It was extremely frustrating, but her gifts of drama and wit were such compensating factors that I do not remember any great sense of irritation. One was simply carried along eagerly listening for the next remark.

Major Gilmour was in bed with flu and unable to fulfil the duties of host that night. So, after supper Mrs Patrick Campbell swept into the lounge in her grand manner and opened his cigar cabinet. With her arms apparently full of these fabulously expensive and very masculine-looking objects, she sailed out of the front door to where the hostess's car and chauffeur were awaiting her.

'Thank you, darling,' she said, as she bid Mrs Gilmour an affectionate good-bye. 'I shall smoke these in bed tonight.'

While Ralph had opened up to us a whole new field of friends and experiences in this world when he brought us to the Cottage, he did not fail to extend our knowledge of communication with the next world while we were there. The Cottage was not only a haven of peace in this world, it was also a centre of psychic power from the Other Side, much as Mrs Leonard's house at Kenley. As we came to know Mrs Gilmour she unfolded the story of her link-up with her own son in the Unseen.

They had, of course, not been interested in such matters until Jim died. There had been one glimpse into the other world at the Cottage years before which had taken her completely by surprise. It was when Jim was still quite a little boy; he became rather seriously ill with scarlet fever, which was in those days a dreaded disease. Mrs Gilmour nursed him herself in her own room, sleeping on a sofa at the foot of the big bed. She became terribly worried at one point, for he seemed to become rapidly worse. She gave him a glass of champagne as a stimulant, and after this he was rather hysterical for a time. When he became quieter she lay down on the sofa thankfully and closed her eyes. After a time she opened them, and to her amazement she saw a monk in a long habit come across the bedroom and stand by the boy's bed for some moments. Then he smiled very kindly at them both and disappeared.

After this Jim slept well for a long time and when he woke he had taken a definite turn for the better.

There seemed to be no connection in their earthly life to account for this visitor, who obviously came to bring healing to the boy. The Gilmours were not Catholics, nor had they any friends or interests in any monastery. What link did the monk have with Jim? Was he someone who had lived in some monastic building on the site before the Cottage was built, or was he perhaps a Guide privileged to help to extend Jim's short spell on earth and who would then be ready to welcome him over there at the proper time?

We found that what Ralph had said about Jim and his own passing being somewhat similar was perfectly true. Jim had been going back to Cambridge, Ralph to Oxford. Jim had changed the date of his departure at the last minute, as had Ralph. Both had died accidentally.

Jim's parents, like Ralph's, had been devastated by their loss. But Jim had succeeded himself in getting through to a friend of Mrs Gilmour's a member of a well-known family whose son was a Cabinet Minister. She was a well-known pioneer in psychic research in those days. The Gilmours were astounded and at first puzzled by the messages, even though they gave considerable evidence of Jim's personal survival, never having thought about this kind of thing before. Then came a phone call from Mrs Latterton, her friend, saying 'Will you take a sitting? I have booked you one with Sir Oliver Lodge's medium.' Mrs Gilmour often told us how she hung on to the phone and hesitated, and then said almost fearfully, 'Yes I will.' There was so much in it for the future had she only known. It was a decision that changed both her and her husband's whole outlook and brought their lives lasting happiness and meaning.

Jim, Major Gilmour told us, had developed his own form of communicaion with them at home by what he called 'Postman's knock'. So that they should not confuse his signals with the ordinary noises that might occur in the house, he always made two knocks close together when he was present.

There was one interesting evening when Mrs Gilmour brought downstairs a wallet in which she kept her first messages, which were very precious to her. She was sitting on a tuffet in the middle of the hearthrug, the wallet open on her knee. As she talked about them to my mother two loud knocks came on the oak box beside the fireplace.

'Ah,' said Major Gilmour, 'that is Jim. He often knocks on that silver mirror over there.'

He had not uttered the words many minutes before two knocks came on the mirror itself as if in answer to his suggestion.

Later, at our sitting at Kenley, Ralph described the scene and said:

> Jim's mother sat on a low seat on the hearth rug, a bit crouched up. She had something open on her knee. Did you know we were rapping? We took it in turns because we were not quite sure if you heard. We kept losing the power and then coming to find you both. You see, when we try to do something like knocking we are very much in your physical conditions, half in and half out, so we feel you in a way physically. I don't mean to say she would have felt me physically, but I was conscious of her and so very close to you. And it gave me quite an absurd feeling when I brushed

against her and said, 'Oh dear, I nearly hurt her.' We laughed about it together.

The obvious presence of an intelligent mind behind these demonstrations of physical phenomena was very clearly portrayed during one lunch which my mother and I took alone together in the Gilmours' dining-room. They were at business all day, so Mrs Gilmour kindly lent us her car to take us to Kenley for our sitting with Gladys Leonard that afternoon.

During lunch the silver candle-sticks on the sideboard and other metal objects were bombarded with 'pings' as if someone who wore a silver thimble was knocking their finger on it. But although these demonstrations of the boys' presence with us were frequent during the meal, they never came while the man-servant was in the room serving a course. Being a very efficient servant, Smith entered the room with a ghost-like smoothness. The silence was broken only by a few formal words of acknowledgement of his services as he removed or set down a plate before us, but not a sound broke the stillness, not a single indiscreet ping from the silver on the sideboard, until he had left the room.

Mrs Gilmour had a strong feeling that the communication was a sacred matter only for herself and her husband and their close friends. She made a point of never speaking of it in front of the servants. It was evidential, therefore, that Jim should respect his mother's wishes so punctiliously and reserve his demonstrations for our ears only. The sound of the rap on the metal was so sharp it could not possibly have gone unnoticed by a third person in that silent room.

When Ian's mother was in London at the same time as we were, the Gilmours would ask her to lunch. Afterwards, the coffee having been served and the servants withdrawn, Ian's mother would employ her gift for turning a table. She used a small round coffee table with a single centre leg and splayed-out feet.

She had amazing psychic power for this form of communication. The table wasted no time in moving, and it was intensely interesting to see the different styles of each communicator. Ian's father, who had been a peer and a famous personality in the legal world, moved it in a slow dignified manner. Ian, a dashing young soldier in a Highland regiment, was far more vigorous and impatient, while Ralph, as the beginner, had nothing like the power and was hesitant and intermittent in his communications.

Jim, apparently, like Ralph, achieved some success of his own in moving things rather in the same manner. Mrs Gilmour had, like my mother, been certain that she had gathered together all his belongings safely after he died. Imagine her surprise therefore when she awoke one morning to find, lying on the top of a file of condolence letters on the desk in her bedroom, an old letter he had written to her himself ages before on returning for a new term to Cambridge. It ran:

> Here I am mummie, alive and well.

How was it that this letter, of all that he had ever written the most appropriate, should have been preserved somewhere out of his mother's sight and suddenly produced as an apt message from the past to convey to her the truth that he was there with her and that he was alive and well, could she but only see him?

6

My father passes to the Unseen

Now that we had become aware of Ralph's constant presence with us in the home, we became even more attached to the house and our local surroundings. My father, who had been failing in health for some time, decided that he must retire. We therefore bought the house, and enlarged it ourselves, the ecclesiastical authorities being only too pleased to sell it and to build an entirely new vicarage nearer the church. We appeared to be becoming more insular. Life in any other place than Dilhorne seemed unthinkable. We little knew how our views and life would change.

A new vicar came and mother settled down to doing much to help him, efforts that made Ralph remark at one sitting that, 'Mummie is becoming quite a wreckagess.' Now this was an amusing piece of evidence, because he used to make a joke about the name of our home by running together the two words for a clergyman's residence, 'vicarage' and 'rectory', and calling the house the Wreckage, but, of course, neither Mrs Leonard nor Feda had ever heard this joke.

My grandmother had passed over meanwhile, leaving us greater financial resources. We were able to afford a car. Our good friend Mrs Bernard (who had seen Ralph on the last day on his way to Oxford), found us a nice young man called Alfred Roberts, whose family she had known for years, who would live in, drive the car and do the housework, an unheard of luxury for us, allowing my mother more time with my father.

Alfred Roberts became indispensable to the family, and his advice and help was elicited on all matters. In fact, a friend once said to me, 'Why, I believe if anyone asked you to marry him, before accepting you would say, "Thanks awfully, I will ask Roberts." '

Unfortunately, though he was supposed to be chauffeur and

house-boy, his duties came to be far more the former than the latter as a result of my mother's capacity for finding people who needed taking out in the car for various urgent reasons, while she herself stayed in and did all the housework. My sarcastic old grandfather wrote one day, 'I shall be very pleased to see you on Tuesday, but don't bring any diseased old women with you needing fresh air!'

In spite of our improved conditions, which benefited my mother, my father's health failed to improve. A case of internal catarrh, which had gone unchecked for too long, had become a chronic disease. He developed jaundice, which became worse and finally affected his heart. We had a deep regret about this illness, for humanly speaking, had the trouble been discovered and treated earlier it could have been placed under control. My father had previously seemed such an exceptionally strong, hardy person.

He took to his bed a little while before Christmas, and passed away one evening on a cold January day after about twelve hours of unconsciousness. I shall always recall that the sunset that night was truly remarkable. Its vivid colour and brilliant light lit the winter sky and a vast sheet of gold poured in at the bedroom window. Strangely enough, it focused on a coloured picture of a cross on a mountain top covered by heather, which hung beside father's bed. A doctor's wife, who called to ask after him at that time and heard he was about to pass, wrote to my mother afterwards, 'Truly the gates of the west stood open for him that night.'

And what of his arrival after he had passed through those gates?

This we were to learn of through the sittings that followed, and what a tremendous joy and comfort those communications were both for my mother and father, as though he had gone on a long journey abroad and had been able to telephone back.

Feda remarked to her in one sitting, 'When you got Ralph back for yourself the important thing was that you got him back for Daddy too.' How true this turned out to be.

> I was with him [Ralph said], holding him and trying to help him so that when once his spirit got out of his sick body

that he had been ill in for so long it got right away. We felt you wanted this too, and this was good because it was better for him not to be with you at first.

They took him to Ralph's house and made him lie down. If Ralph had to leave him, there was someone else whom he knew beside him in case he awoke. If he did, they just told him to go to sleep again, because after all that suffering he must get used to the new life quietly. His sleep was different from our sleep. It was a kind of conscious unconsciousness, like one sometimes gets in the early morning when one knows there is someone there.

He felt rather better some little time before he passed, and this had been arranged by Ralph so that he could leave a happier phase and memory behind him. This made a better setting for him on the Other Side.

When he asked Ralph about his death later, Ralph only said, 'Put your fingers in your mouth and feel your nice teeth.'

This was very evidential to us, as he hated his false teeth. In fact it was putting off having his decayed teeth taken out that probably created the cararrh and toxic condition which caused his passing.

'We help him to go slowly and get accustomed to his new body,' Ralph explained, 'because it was different from my passing. I passed quickly, and was used to having a sound body here. Daddy had to get used to having a body that is light and well.'

'I wish you could see him,' Ralph said. 'He has got a nice pink in his cheeks and looks much younger. He was so amazed to hear again.' Ralph did not just communicate with him by thought, as he could have done, but spoke deliberately, because he thought his father would like to hear his voice again and realize he was not deaf.

'It seems so extraordinary to hear the birds, and the music,' father had said.

This was very evidential, as one of the things he had missed most when he went deaf as a youngish man was hearing the nightingales at Oxford.

'He is so pleased with himself and Ralph has been showing

him everything and introducing him to all the people he has got to know over there,' Feda added.

> Sometimes, you know, even though Daddy loved people, he liked to toddle off a bit by himself as if he drew something from it. Even here, on the Other Side, Ralph will miss him sometimes, but Ralph does not worry, he has just gone scouting around seeing how the land lies and he will come back and say what he has seen.

This habit was so typical of Daddy, though it was quite unknown to Mrs Leonard. He had such a capacity for rushing off on a voyage of discovery, even when we were all on a journey together, filling the family with apprehension. He always turned up again, however, in some extraordinary way, even if it was jumping into the last carriage as the train moved out of a station we had stopped at *en route*. Then he would walk leisurely through to join us in our carriage, where, owing to the delay, we had quite given up hope of seeing him and were quite sure he had been left behind this time.

Feda said that Daddy was very pleased with Ralph's house. Things like nice belongings and charming houses always pleased him. There were long windows, open, not at the broad but at the narrow part. There were two steps down and then a grass slope in terraces, because my mother liked them, he said. (Certainly they had them at her old home.) There was a lovely rock garden near the house; he had designed the house himself: it was a little like the one we had on earth, but there were all kinds of improvements he had thought of himself.

He found it a strange way to travel by flying to places, but he went with Ralph at first to gain confidence. He said it was like learning to skate.

Ralph went on to say that he and his father had been to call on Jim's mother early one morning as she awoke, as she had been with them on the Other Side. They hoped they might help her to bring the memory back, and made a big knock. Although Mrs Seymour had no recollection of her journey on the Other Side, she was able to substantiate the story by telling us she was awakened by this loud knock, just as they said.

After alluding to this episode, Feda went on:

> Ralph and his father think you will be more in London later on; it seems as if they will be helping you to do that because his father has got a strange feeling that there is some work for you to do in connection with this, and now he is on the Other Side he will be able to help you with it.

At the end of the second sitting after my father's passing, an exciting and quite unexpected thing happened—unexpected it seemed even to Feda, although it concerned her so closely. She had just been giving a long message direct from my father concerning his dogs and his life with them over there, when suddenly she said, 'Oh dear, he is losing it, isn't it nuisance?' (meaning, one presumed, the power to speak through her). Then she continued, 'It is to you he is speaking, you know he says all I feel.'

There was a pause, and then suddenly in a clear distinct whisper came another voice from Gladys Leonard's mouth, saying urgently:

'Come closer. I can't quite make you hear me. My own darling I can't quite make you hear me distinctly. I cannot speak loudly at all. I am so happy.'

'I can hear you,' my mother replied encouragingly, suddenly recognizing the familiar voice.

Then my father's voice continued, 'You know what it all means to me. Don't worry about anything; it is all quite safe here. I told you it would be. Good-bye.'

'Good-bye darling,' my mother replied.

'He just whispered a few words,' Feda added.

'He spoke most distinctly,' my mother replied.

Across the typescript she has added in her own writing:

> My husband took complete control and spoke in his own voice exactly.

Few people controlled Gladys Leonard besides Feda. It is interesting to note that even Feda did not appear to know that he was about to make this effort, as she had expressed the view that he was losing the power when it would seem that it was really she herself who was losing contact with the medium so that Daddy could come through.

Feda appeared to take control of Gladys again in a moment, and when my mother said to her, 'How wonderful it was to hear his voice,' she replied as if it had been planned in a general way, 'He knew it would be if he managed to get it, and he says again, give you all his love, everything is quite safe, don't worry about anything.'

The next time this occurred it seemed that Feda had come to some more definite arrangement about my father coming through before the sitting, for she broke off a message she was giving about someone else and said, 'All right Daddy I am not forgetting you.' Then she turned to us and said, 'Daddy is pretending not to look anxious, but he is. He is trying to be polite, but he is afraid I will use the power and there will be none left for him.'

Then Feda made a very interesting gesture to establish my father's undoubted identity before he took control. Mrs Leonard always wrapped herself in a soft warm plaid rug before the sitting, as she was apt to go rather cold when in trance. Imagine our alarm, therefore, when we saw Feda deliberately unwrap it and carefully tear a wide strip off such a valuable possession. Having got the piece free, she took hold of the two ends and threw the loose part behind her, arranging it across her shoulders in the shape of a hood. It was only when we saw the arrangement complete that we realized she had made a perfect imitation of a clergyman's M.A. hood. My father was rather old-fashioned in the robes he wore in Church, and he continued to wear his hood long after most clergymen had given up using them on ordinary occasions. But he had never taken a service within hundreds of miles of where Mrs Leonard lived. She had only ever seen him wearing a dark-grey clerical suit. She could not possibly have known any details of the robes he wore in church. Feda made no comment on her action, feeling so sure, I suppose, of its significance. She just quietly withdrew.

This time we were ready, after the initial pause, for his delighted cry, 'I am coming, darling. I am coming. Are you there and is Ruth there too? I am trying to come, dearest.' The voice was typical of him. When he took control, Mrs Leonard's features also seemed to change, her wide, rather uneven mouth with fairly full lips, became flat and thin just like my father's ecclesiastical one.

On this second occasion there was a terribly high wind outside, which made it difficult to hear his voice. He remarked on this without our having to explain the difficulty, so he was evidently well aware of conditions around us on earth at that moment.

Then he grasped my mother's hand and said:

> Isn't it wonderful to be holding your hand again dearest, it is so strange I seem to be using Gladys like a sort of machine.
>
> I am so glad I can talk to you myself. It is perfectly right, of course, what Feda says about me and Ralph. I like her to tell you what she thinks about me too sometimes, then you know she sees me as I am.

Speaking of constantly being with my mother, he referred especially to All Saints' Day, a festival which had fallen shortly before the sitting, and said, 'I am constantly with you, especially when you go to bed, because it is a quiet and peaceful time, and always when you pray.'

As time went on my father was able to hold a conversation of quite ten minutes with us in a fairly strong voice, though it never achieved the strength of Feda's. Mostly he gave his own quiet comments, as he would have done in earth life, on what she had said, often in a typical way, but not having the great amount of power which Feda had, nor her life-long rapport with Gladys Leonard, he was not capable of taking on a whole sitting. But the feeling of personal contact and affection he achieved well justified these brief contacts.

We were interested to learn something of my father's new work. Mr Drayton Thomas kindly took a proxy sitting for us. When he asked him if he had preached any sermons since he went over, and if there was any scope for them, my father replied 'There is indeed an alarming amount of scope. At one time on earth I should have imagined that those entering the kingdom of Heaven or the After Life would have no use for them, but I find they are more needed than they were on earth or [and he smiled here, Feda commented] and more greatly appreciated.'

'Do you use them from your previous collection or make new ones?' Mr Drayton Thomas asked.

> My old collections [father replied], but working them out from the point of view we had on earth supplanted with the fuller light we have here on the same subjects. The ones who need the sermons are, of course, the newcomers. We must not forget that they are arriving in their thousands daily, and the majority of people, I regret to say, are unenlightened, quite unenlightened. I had hoped that those who would need the simpler form of instruction which we had on earth would be in the minority, but it was not so. It is our fault, because what we have given them on earth did not amount to very much. It has not answered all their hidden doubts and fears and their subconscious difficulties. Ministers and pastors have not understood their difficulties, even if we have half felt them, we have not always known what would adequately meet their needs. Even those who are apparently indifferent have had their time when they wanted help and perhaps come to our Churches hoping for it, but have been given the proverbial stone. If we had only given them from the pulpit what we know now to be the facts of existence, the facts of eternal life. We know now that the greatest human need is to know what is behind this great calamity, this great crisis that faces us all—death. It is the dark shadow that falls across our brightest days on earth, and if we could give them quietly and naturally a little light on that subject I think the churches would be more than full, for I think that the majority of people still look to the pastors of the flock for guidance.

Mr Drayton Thomas also asked my father if he had seen Christ, to which Feda replied:

> He says 'Yes, it has been my privilege to see Him.' [Feda then added], 'He is not saying anything about it, just bowing his head. 'I have only just recently visited that plane,' he

says. 'When some of them go for the first time they often cannot speak of it for a while. I think it takes some time to somehow gather up all they feel about it. I think it is rather different from what they expected. It is for most people.

Ralph himself had remarked to us in a previous sitting: 'We can visit the Christ Sphere when one's sensitivity is employed.' And added, 'Life is more glorious over here than I had ever imagined. How can mortal bodies visualize the immortal?'

7

The pattern of individual destiny and spiritual links

As the years went by I came to feel that our communications did not only bring us conviction of survival, interesting messages and new friends. They also brought us revelations of the Divine purpose, the pattern of an individual destiny in life in relation to God's plan. This, of course, was particularly emphasized in the messages concerning my brother's passing, but it was not only this one isolated event which revealed a pattern of intended purpose. The most diverse events were later to build up into an apparent pattern showing how one thing had led to another, though they might be years apart in physical time.

When my father went over to the Other Side, he remarked in one sitting that the two matters he felt he should have paid more attention to were, first, the Blessed Virgin Mary, and secondly, the importance of animals. He did not qualify these ideas at the time with further detail, but, as so often happens, the pattern of destiny contained in these two diverse subjects was slowly to work out for me.

But first I must return to the earlier part of my brother's life, for its importance regarding subsequent events and because it was through them especially that I came to understand what had seemed a totally unfulfilled part of his life.

For Ralph there had been only one girl who had ever attracted him. Their friendship began when, as a little boy of eight, he had first met her at a dancing class where he always made her his partner. As he grew up and met other girls he did not change in the least; in fact his attachment grew stronger. Like most of the really important loyalties of his life, he expressed it in a quietly unobtrusive way, but it went very deep.

I recall that my mother spoke to me one day about it when I was quite a child and made me promise never to tease Ralph or gossip to my friends about it, because she said it was such a very deep affection. This promise I always kept.

Her name was Mildred and her father was a doctor—a fact which may have shaped his career by influencing his decision to become one himself. He was the third generation in a family practice, a remarkable man and deeply beloved in the neighbourhood. For us it was quite a precedent to have a doctor in the family, though there was said to be a possible connection with the famous Lord Lister through my great-grandfather whose name was Anthony Heward Lister and who also came from Yorkshire. Almost prophetically Ralph had been christened Ralph Lister Plant. With his quiet, sympathetic manner, great conscientiousness and analytical mind, he was ideally suited to this profession.

My mother used to try and persuade him to make his affection more known to Mildred. Looking back over these years, having seen the jealousy and possessiveness many doting mothers show when their child, especially a son, chooses a life partner, I realize how wonderfully liberal and unselfish my mother was in this. She wished only that Ralph should have his happiness fulfilled. My father, for his part, had no objection to Ralph marrying a Roman Catholic. He was tolerant to *all* Churches outside his own.

Mildred was outstandingly attractive, brilliant at tennis and all the social activities of our day. At dances she could have booked her programme twice over. She had beautiful features and men admired her for this and her quiet poise and peaceful assurance. My mother feared she would be snapped up by one of them before becoming aware of Ralph's affection. But, in those days, conscientious young men did not propose until they could offer 'prospects', and Ralph was only a medical student.

He, on his part, refused to be alarmed by this suggestion, as was his attitude towards most of things we got apprehensive about. He always evinced a calm trust that things would work out for the best. When my mother became agitated he would merely smile and say gently, 'All will be well,' and again 'All will be well.' We did not then realize that this was the saying of the famous mystic, Dame Julian of Norwich.

It was only later that we became aware of how true his words were and how the Divine plan was working out the best for both of them, though not in the way we envisaged in our earthly minds.

As time went on, Mildred's mother began to realize that she was becoming rather elusive about long-term plans for the future, as she afterwards told my mother, and she wondered why. Mildred seemed to be thinking of something else beyond the day-to-day activities of ordinary life. Then it became apparent that she was developing a vocation to be a nun. Through all the busy life and gaiety in the world, the conviction grew that God's particular purpose in life was for her to serve him through the power of prayer in a contemplative order. This may seem strange to those who have never known a nun personally, the popular idea being that they are usually drawn from dreamy idealists or girls disappointed in love. Such characters would never have the self-discipline and spiritual resources necessary for that life. It is those who have loved life who are most capable of falling in love with God.

Six weeks after my brother died, Mildred, her mind now made up, entered the Carmelite Order, and the pattern of their two lives on this earth was complete. Looked at solely from the level of this world, it seems to make no sense. Ralph was all his days in love with a girl whom he would never marry, his destiny to end his life on the brink of his medical career. But the view is utterly changed once we see over the horizon into the next world. These two did not require the tie of physical marriage and an earthly life together. They were already deeply linked and their paths could deviate on a journey. She would reach the higher spheres through a life of active prayer here on earth, he by an early passing through the gates of death. No doubt they will meet again in the immeasurable years of eternity that are before them.

Our link with the family did not end there, for it was not without great purpose in my life also. It was just another example of the threads running through our lives and linking together the apparently most diverse events which have great significance for our knowledge and development.

Sometime after Mildred entered the convent her father died suddenly from heart failure while attending a patient. His funeral, a Requiem Mass, was held at the Catholic church in a nearby town. We knew the building well by sight, having often seen his car standing outside when we went shopping. Though his life was very busy as a doctor, he seemed to find time to go there frequently to pray. Now we entered the church for the first time. I had been in few Catholic churches before, and had certainly never attended a Requiem Mass. I do not remember much of the service; it seemed rather elaborate and bewildering then, though the general atmosphere of the church and the occasion may have heightened my susceptibilities to inner experiences.

When we came out to follow the procession to the cemetery, the most amazing sight greeted us. The streets were lined with people. It seemed as though everyone in the town had turned out to speed this beloved figure on his last journey. There were people of every class and creed, from black-coated workers to 'throwers' straight from the potter's wheel, their white overalls covered in potters' clay.

As we walked up the road my awareness grew of a strange impression. This was no ordinary crowd, come out to view the funeral of a well-known person so as not to miss something of local interest. It was a group completely caught up in a profound communal sense, an act of reverence in which all participated like the thoughts in a gigantic mind. Suddenly I became aware of the great power of unity at this higher level, and of how group faith, if carried to its logical conclusion, might indeed move mountains.

Realizing it was a long walk to the cemetery and that we should really have brought the car, we tried to attract the attention of our own doctor, whose car, driven by his chauffeur, was passing alongside us at little more than walking pace. Even though he sat as an inactive passenger, he was staring ahead of him in a strange reverie, and seemed unable to heed our efforts.

Therefore we reached the cemetery a little late. The family were already observing the last graveside rites of a Catholic funeral. Each mourner in turn dipped a gold brush in a receptacle and sprinkled a liquid on the coffin. In those days I did not even know that this was Holy Water. Probably I thought it was incense, as I associated this with Catholic practices. As we stood there, one of the doctor's relatives, a young girl of whose flippancy I did not approve, stepped forward and sprinkled the coffin. My immediate reaction was one of indignation that anyone so superficial should undertake such a task. I felt her efforts could be of no value whatsoever.

Then, suddenly, I received an impression which overrode all my personal reactions and previous ideas. It was almost as if a voice had spoken to me from the Unseen. I became strongly aware that the qualities of the person fulfilling such an act were not important. They were merely like the tap conveying the water. The act itself liberated vast unseen forces, like power conveyed by an electric cable. I did not only know this intuitively, but even felt it in some way flowing down.

Thinking this over logically, I came to realize the active power present in ancient rites, but especially in the great historic ceremonies of the Church—a hot-line, as it were, to Heaven through the centuries.

Such ideas were not previously in my mind. My father was what would be called a broad Church of England clergyman. He was critical of the rather self-conscious ritual practised by some of the 'spiky' Anglo-Catholic clergy who lived around and who were so concerned with ritual that they appeared to practise it only for ritual's sake—doing the done thing, like social manners. In fact, when one of our old parishioners moved into one of their parishes and described his new vicar as 'being full of monkey tricks in Church', my father very much enjoyed the joke.

I do not recall my father ever making any special pronouncement on the relationship of the service and the quality of the clergyman. I had grown up with a general impression that you should not turn your back lightly on your church if there was some slight controversy with the vicar, but that to go to one where the vicar was not 'nice' would considerably negate the spiritual value.

This episode at the grave was therefore all the more surprising, since it caused me completely to reverse my views through an instant conviction which seemed outside myself. How did the new belief reach me? It was, of course, something intended for me by God, but on looking back over the years I feel that it may have been conveyed by a close spiritual entity, of whose character and personality I shall say more later.

The whole episode of the funeral somehow seemed to heighten my sensitivity and caused me to pass into a state which might without exaggeration be called a spiritual ecstasy.

It is very difficult to speak of such personal religious experiences in a way that is intelligible or even interesting to others. I cannot, for myself, even resuscitate the actual feeling of joy or revive extraordinary experiences once they are past. This, of course, only makes them seem the more real, since they were things beyond my ken, merely given to me for a period and then withdrawn; or, I am afraid it may be more accurate to say, forfeited as I slowly descended from the spiritual heights back to my level. All I can remember was that a great humility was the corner-stone of the whole experience. That is, a positive humility which deprived the evils of pride and self-will of their power; it was not the humility preoccupied with personal guilt, the post-mortem discussion of each little individual sin which is a sort of luxury commodity for the over-pious. But perhaps we should term that self-pity rather than humility. It is so difficult to discuss things in the spiritual sphere in words.

To express my feelings, at this time and to put something on record about them, I wrote in my Bible a prayer which I still have. It consisted of these few lines:

> What joy to live near Jesus to put ourselves into his hand, to be constantly looking up to him any moment of the night or day with great joy but *extreme humility*.

The characteristic of this experience was the wholeness of the act of giving oneself, the complete and spontaneous identification with Christ through free will, passing into a state in which free will seemed to lose its power. It had sprung into reality through our friend's life on earth, I suppose, but this had in turn touched off for me something of spiritual contact with higher sources.

I wrote a letter to a friend at this time, which I never posted. It runs:

> It is very difficult to describe my feelings but somehow the great thing is growing. I am beginning to realize why people

were so willing to do all kinds of things for Christ, even to give their lives for him, because they had 'fallen in love', as it were, with God.

The focus of my devotions at this time was a small hand-done Christmas card which resembled a page from an illuminated MS. It had been given to me by Mildred's sister who was Reverend Mother to a Carmelite convent. It was made by her nuns, and I had it framed and put it by my bedside when I said my prayers. At the top was a round portrait in a scroll setting of a lady in a blue veil, and behind her a glimpse of a wonderful landscape: a valley with poplar tress and wild flowers stretching away up to blue mountains. Under the picture was written:

> In me is all grace of the way and of the truth, in me is all hope of life and virtue. I have blossomed forth as a rose planted by the brooks of water. Ecclus. XXXIX.

So unversed was I at this time in anything Catholic, that I failed to realize the identity of the lady in the blue veil, or the landscape behind her. I never even noticed her halo. I looked on the picture as a pious decoration to the text, imagining that the words referred to the coming of Christ, as they resembled some of the prophesies in Isaiah and wondering why they were not from that particular book. Having read the statement over I felt so profoundly uplifted that the need to make some sort of response became strong, and as if in answer I would say, 'Yes verily and indeed I know it and I know you are worthy to be praised.' I thought I was addressing Christ, not knowing who the subject was portrayed in the picture.

This is another of those strange indications of a long thread of continuity, for it was only thirty years later, when I went to Lourdes on a pilgrimage for animal welfare, that I awoke to the full meaning of the text and the real identity of the person. There over the door of the Church at the Grotto, I read it again: a prophecy that had gone out hundreds of years before, foretelling the appearance of Our Lady to St Bernadette in a grotto with roses round her feet by the stream at Masebele. When I thought of all the miracles that had taken place over the ensuing years, and saw the vast healing spring she had caused to burst forth, and which still pours gallons down the hillside day and night, I realized the importance of the words and how indeed she had 'blossomed forth like a rose by the brooks of water'.

Not only there at Lourdes, but all my life, she has blossomed in innumerable and extraordinary ways, instantly answering prayers of all kinds, bringing amazing healing to seriously ill friends and peace to the dying. No wonder my father sent back a message over the importance of contacting her.

We each undoubtedly have personalities in the Unseen—call them Guides, or what you will—who help and influence our lives and of whose presences we may sometimes be allowed to become aware. I learnt a good deal about one of mine as time went on, and this helped me to understand something of the source of my spiritual inspiration and help as well as the shape in which it came.

As our communications continued, many psychics began to tell me about a higher spiritual person who seemed to be near to me and concerned to help with my work. Sometimes they saw him with his hand on my shoulder, as if taking care of me, sometimes on my head in blessing. They were not necessarily spiritual psychics who saw him, which made it all the more evidential as their minds would not contain a mental picture of any such person.

The most remarkable admission of his presence came when two friends invited me to their flat for a 'reading' from a clairvoyant they had engaged who practised crystal-gazing. These friends were both men researchers, and they made the appointment as a business arrangement without ever having met the clairvoyant personally or gossipped to her about me in advance.

She proved highly suitable for this kind of arrangement. The moment she arrived she explained, in no uncertain terms, that she 'did not have anything to do with that spiritualistic lot'. She did not get in touch with spirits, she said; her chief function seemed advising people over business investments, for which she was apparently well known. She told us how once, when one of her regular clients booked an appointment, he was preceded by the two men he was contemplating making a deal with. They offered her £200 to say the deal was a good one and their company sound. Luckily the lady (who told us the story to illustrate the temptations of her profession) refused the bribe. When her real client arrived and she went into the matter psychically, she discovered that the firm 'had not' as she described it 'even enough to pay the postage stamps in its resources'.

It was therefore extremely surprising that, when she came to me, her whole attitude changed. Without realizing that, in her excitement, she was contradicting her previous observations she exclaimed, 'When I come to you I feel such an overwhelming presence of a spiritual kind that I must speak of it, it is so clear.'

After further conversation about this wonderful influence, she peered into the crystal and became very excited by what she saw.

'Oh,' she cried. 'Something is building up. It is a figure on a pedestal, and it is entirely in gold. Look!' I jumped up from my chair and peered over her shoulder into the crystal, and there I caught a glimpse of it. The figure of a fairly tall man on a pedestal, and it was suffused with golden light.

Near the flat where this took place there was a statue of the person who was my constant companion from the Unseen, the overshadowing presence that even she felt; but the clairvoyant had no idea of this, nor of his identity. It was only some years after we first began hearing of him through psychics that we ourselves realized his identity. My mother and I often talked the matter over, wondering whom he could be.

The first reference I can trace in a Leonard sitting came apparently when Feda stated that there were two men trying to get through, and she asked to be excused if she referred to one as 'the ordinary man', to distinguish him, she went on to say, 'from the wonderful old man who is here'. The wonderful one did writings, did he not do some preachings too? she asked.

> I don't know whether he was an ordinary clergyman. He is standing behind Ruth and putting his hands on her head. I feel as if he was an old man when he passed over, but he has got very much younger now. Ralph [she added] says he was a saint when he was here. I get a feeling of people calling him Father. I don't think I have got him before.

In the sitting record our notetaker has typed in the observation '(Not placed)'.

As mentioned earlier my upbringing had taken place in a very broad Church atmosphere. The fact that Cardinal Newman was first cousin to my grandmother had not registered on me. My father had always had a great respect for Newman, but he was critical of those of his contemporaries who adhered to the form of Anglo-Catholicism then current. So far as historical figures went in the ecclesiastical field, it was Charles Kingsley, the Anglican clergyman (author of *The Water Babies*) with whom Newman entered into intellectual controversy (and as a result of which he wrote his famous book *The Apologia*) of whom we heard most in the family. It never entered my head, therefore, that this person so constantly mentioned was my famous cousin, and that he was in a sense my guide and helper.

It was through another great spiritual influence in my life that I came to recognize the identity of my cousin. I was still at school when I first heard Father Basil Jellicoe speak. He was an Anglican priest who was to become famous for his onslaught on the slums. The impact of his personality was tremendous. Though a convinced Catholic of the Anglican variety, he had none of the 'spiky' tendencies of our other Anglo-Catholic contacts. Perhaps this was because he was permeated with a sense of realism. When he joined the church we attended in London, St Martin-in-the-Fields, some of his High Church colleagues raised their eyebrows at his departure from the Anglo-Catholic to a 'liberal' sphere and said, 'They don't reserve the sacrament there.' 'No,' he replied, 'but they reserve the crypt for the down-and-outs.'

This was the time of the great slump, and his sense of urgency over social problems and his firm adherence to leading Catholic principles bridged for us the gap which had seemed to separate the two. It was through him that we discovered the church of All Saints, Margaret Street, particularly alive in those days under the influence of a much-beloved vicar, Don Bernard Clements. I shall never forget the first night we stepped inside for the Benediction, and saw the candles blazing on the High Altar in gloriously wrought silver candle-sticks against a background of brilliant red hangings. It was not only the grandeur of the scene. There was a point of spiritual focus, a 'hot-line' to the higher spheres.

It was then, during the singing of the hymn 'Praise to the Holiest', that I received the answer to my frequent question, who was my great spiritual guide? 'Praise to the Holiest' is a chorus from Newman's great poem *The Dream of Gerontius*, which Sir Edward Elgar made into his greatest oratorio. I had never heard of the poem then, and only knew the words as an Anglican hymn of which Newman was author. It was exquisitely rendered by the boys of the famous resident choir school attached to the church. As their voices soared it suddenly came to me. I whispered to my mother, 'I know who the saintly old gentleman with me is. It is Cardinal Newman!'

As time went on there were many references to him in communications, though his surname was never given, which made it the more evidential, for the medium could hardly have thought by chance of a particular famous man and conned his life up from a book. If a name was given, he was generally referred to as 'your cousin John'. We identified him also from intimate references to details of the French Huguenot family from which his mother and my grandmother came. Relations mentioned were also people from the past, whom we found on the family tree.

The main purpose of his coming, however, seemed to be to indicate his nearness to give his blessing, and to bring encouragement to me in my writing. 'He wrote books himself and he wants Ruth to carry on the torch,' Feda said.

In an early sitting, where I was fumbling over the idea of writing this book, he gave me these words of encouragement and useful criticism.

> He is with Ruth [Feda said], and he wants her to exercise her writing gift. She has to get it in order by herself more. He will help her when she has done this. They tried to impress this on her from the Other Side recently. There seem to be other things coming in and interrupting but it is a gift and they want her to make time for it. The book is like a sandwich at present, it wants filling. The fat part in the middle will stick it together. You have got good material, but don't force it, you have got stale over it.

Who could better understand the latter problem than the Cardinal, who in spite of his inherent brilliance got only a pass at Oxford as a result of over-working in his undergraduate days.

> Write up a bit of the episodes in sittings how they helped you, and make it an interesting recital for bereaved people. When you have done this you will strengthen the middle part of the book better [the instructions continued].

At a clairvoyance given by Mrs Ursula Roberts during a conference arranged by the Churches Fellowship for Psychic and Spiritual Study at Long Melford Vicarage, he again gave a message of encouragement.

Mrs Roberts said, 'I see an old clergyman with a funny little silver hat, there is a doctor link and a schoolmaster one too. He is carrying a sheaf of MS to do with writing a book. I feel the person to whom the message is addressed is helping with writing a book.'

Newman was, of course, known as Dr Newman in his Anglican days, and had many posts as tutor.

'He stands with his hand on your shoulder,' she went on. 'I see the pages of the MS fluttering over. He says You have not gone back. You were worried about this.'

'Yes,' I replied, 'I was.'

'Well tell her it is all right, she has not gone back.'

My cousin made an unexpected appearance through Mrs Allingham, a medium who belonged to the Churches Fellowship, when he suddenly appeared to her before her home circle one day. She had neither met nor heard of me then, so when her sitting assembled she asked the members if any of them had any connection with the Cardinal. Mrs Pollard, a friend of mine who was present, told Mrs Allingham she knew someone who was his cousin, and so I was invited to the circle. This time she saw the Cardinal again, and he showed her a reddish-brown book and said, 'It is in the book.'

I realized that he was alluding to a copy of *The History of My Religious Opinions*, one of his own books that he had given to my grandmother. But I did not realize the full significance until later, when I received a further message from him through Mrs

Ursula Roberts at another Churches Fellowship Conference. This took the shape of a book text.

Mrs Roberts began by saying that she saw there a clergyman with one of those funny old-fashioned flat hats, who was fond of Tintern Abbey. She then added, 'He wrote a collection of sermons that were published.'

My father was very fond of Tintern Abbey, and as he wore an old-fashioned flat hat of black straw when he went cycling there in the summer, I took it to mean him, though the sermons were Newman's. It seems likely that my father and our cousin came together to the group, and as they were standing close together, the medium confused their conditions, as can happen so easily when there is a crowd at a large clairvoyance; or possibly Newman, shunning any publicity, wished to send his objective piece of evidence, which spoke for itself, through my father, who being less famous would attract less comment.

The message appeared to have some strange connection with a man sitting about four chairs away from me; in fact at first Mrs Roberts thought that it was for him, though he was unable to place it. The reason for this link I was to learn later.

The message ran that I had at home a book written by the communicator. He wanted to say that if I opened it at page 76, column two, I should find a message for the work now being undertaken (i.e. in the Churches Fellowship whose conference it was).

Anxiously I hurried home and took out the copy of *The History of My Religious Opinions* which Cardinal Newman had given to my grandmother. It was inscribed in his sensitive, frail handwriting, 'Antoinette S. Plant from her affectionate cousin John H. Newman. Dec. 8th 1871.' I turned over the pages and read from the place indicated. This is what I found.

> From beginnings so small, from elements of thought so fortuitous, with prospects so unpromising, the party suddenly became a power in the National Church, and an object of alarm to her rulers and friends. Its originators would have found it difficult to say what they aimed at of a practical kind; rather they put forth views and principles for their own sake, because they were true, as if they were obliged to say them;

> and they might themselves be surprised at their earnestness in uttering them, they had as greater cause to be surprised at the success which attended their propagation. And in fact they could only say that those doctrines were in the air: that to assert was to prove, and to explain was to persuade; and that the movement in which they were taking part was the birth of a crisis rather than of a place. In a very few years a school of opinion was formed, fixed in its principles, indefinite and progressive in range, and it expended itself into every part of the country.

The original purpose of this paragraph was, of course, to describe the efforts by Newman and his friends to bring back to the Church of England the mystical and Catholic beliefs mistakenly thrown out in the heat of the Reformation. Now it appeared amazingly appropriate for our own efforts to extend further a knowledge of the Unseen and mystical thought through the Churches' Fellowship for Psychic and Spiritual Studies: approaches especially appropriate to our present age.

The medium was an active Spiritualist who had never studied Catholic doctrine or Newman's works. I had never had a private sitting with her when I might have spoken of these matters. When the message came through, she did not at first realize it was for me, but thought it was for my neighbour.

The quotation seems beautifully apt and tremendously appropriate to our situation. Surely it shows an intelligent mind with great literary taste and an intimate knowledge of the book. Was it therefore not likely that it had indeed been chosen by the author himself?

After the lecture I found the link with my neighbour, Mr Roberts. When I mentioned who my cousin was, he said at once that he had just read a book about Newman and had felt drawn to him. He wanted very much to learn more about him. When he got a book by the Cardinal soon after, he wrote me of a further link realized between them, as Newman never meditated without a pencil in his hand, a thing which Mr Roberts did also.

Later on I toyed with the idea of a home circle of my own, so decided to hold a sitting at which I could try to get in touch with my cousin John only and ask him his opinion about receiving his help in this. I therefore chose to approach an entirely fresh medium who had never brought him through before—a man medium whom I thought would be fairly objective in his messages and not be influenced by feelings for or against such a famous figure.

I took with me my grandmother's copy of Newman's book, covered in brown paper so that it was not in the least possible for him to have identified it with the human eye. I gave it to him at once so that he could focus on the person whom I hoped would come through.

It proved a most interesting sitting. The identity of my cousin was completely established by references to the French Huguenot family from which he and my grandmother had come, while other relatives were mentioned and references made to the book. Only half-way through the sitting the medium asked, 'Why do I see a Cardinal?' I then explained that the communicator was one himself, though I did not state which Cardinal

After this I put the salient question to my cousin. 'Tell him,' I said to the medium, 'I am thinking of starting a home circle. If I do this, would he like to be the guide of it?' To this Newman gave a definite, 'No.'

I pursued the matter further by saying that our intentions in inviting him were because he might possibly have some teaching he would like to give, new angles on the old truths which he may have learnt since he went over there. His reply was:

> The poor world is full of teaching. What it wants is to learn how to live it. Since I came over here I have learnt that I can help people on the earth in a way I did not realize before. I am one of a band of helpers and I do not want my name attached to any one particular task. What does it matter so long as the work gets done?

I think this utterance proves that neither my mind nor the medium's had any influence on the message. First, I would have welcomed him warmly as a guide to our circle and the medium would have been only too glad to claim such a famous person for the movement. As he did not know the identity of the

Cardinal, he might have expected such an important person to reject or accept the idea on grounds of pride, but not to reply in such a self-effacing way, which I realize was so characteristic of this greatly beloved figure. Those who have made a close study of Newman's works have said that this utterance was typical of him and his great modesty, though I was not then aware of this. The knowledge of his nearness and blessing and the support of his band of helpers are a constant source of spiritual power in my daily life. I have respected his wish to shun the more collective and tangible which might lead to unwanted praise, and even false messages as a result of his famous name.

Perhaps this is why, even though his case has been put forward to Rome for canonization, there have been no miracles or manifestations or other assets to promote the cause. Newman, in his great modesty and spiritual happiness, prefers to remain a faithful but anonymous servant of God working from the Unseen.

8

The place of animals in the creation

Apart from my father's personal reference to animals, and their new significance for him on the Other Side, this book would not be complete without some reference to them because, when we begin thinking consistently in terms of total harmony and wholeness of life, we cannot leave them out and we begin to see them from a different aspect from how a normally conventional upbringing has shown them. Even in Britain, where animals are kept in many homes, people still tend to think of them as pleasant additions to a family's assets, much like a good car or a ciné camera. In the case of a pedigree dog or a horse they may even be a mere status symbol.

Even those who really do love animals seem to find it necessary to cloak the fact with some such remark as, 'Of course, you know, I am afraid I am sentimental about animals.' They do not seem to realize that what they should be saying is, 'Of course, you know, I am really consistent about this idea of total love and harmony, I love animals too.' How irrelevant apologetics of this kind sound in a so-called Christian country, supposed to subscribe to a concept of universal love.

Those who wish to keep free of any entanglements in the field of animal awareness generally apply the well-worn cliché, 'Ah, but you see, children must come first.' They seem to be perpetually imagining themselves in a situation which does not occur in Western civilization, thank God: that of possessing only one last crust of bread and having to choose between giving it to their child or their dog.

The warmth of love that both children and animals naturally long for and need is a limitless commodity. There is plenty for both if we will only make the personal effort of caring enough to express it. Why should we curtail love in order to exclude a part of God's creation which asks so little and gives so much?

It was Jerome K. Jerome who wrote appropriately, 'What a foolish friend a dog is. He never asks if you are going up or down life's ladder, stupid or wise sinner or saint. You are his friend and he is going to stick to you come good fortune or bad, even if need be give his life for you, silly brainless soulless dog.'

I always find it strange that those who subscribe to the opinion that animals have no souls use the idea to justify an argument that animals are thus of no consequence. Surely if they have no souls, then we must regard all the love and devotion that emanates from them as of even greater importance, for being designated creatures of a lower order, how can love be in them unless God put it there himself?

The first revelation about men's illogical thinking towards animals came when I was about five years old. We had a pet cockerel called Harry of the grey Plymouth Rock variety, fashionable in those days. He came from a hen's egg that one of my pet bantams had been given to hatch, and was a bit of an odd man out. It was therefore suggested that as he was rather superfluous, Nannie should catch Harry and a man would call and take him to market. I agreed because I did not then realize that this was in reality sending him to his death. Nannie explained that I should not like to help her catch Harry, but I felt I should try to be like other people and take things of this kind as a part of normal life. So although my instinct was against it, I decided to help.

I remember that after an agonizing chase round the yard we finally cornered the shrieking Harry in the black inferno of the coal cellar. By then I could no longer countenance such appalling treachery to a friend, and ran to Nannie begging her to let him go. But she thrust him into a big tub with a lid that stood there, saying the man would soon call and take him to market. She also added, I remember, that I should not have helped as she had said that it would not be nice.

Nannie's solution did not satisfy me at all; merely to turn one's back on something like this, because it was not nice, did not solve anything. I began to think the matter over, and suddenly I saw the objective truth. Why should Harry, who had learnt to trust us and who looked to us for food and shelter, be suddenly attacked and hounded to his death. Wasn't it a piece of blatant barbarism on the part of us—the so-called civilized occupants of the world. Phrases like 'chicken is so delicious' had been built up over the years to pad the corners of reality for the stupid and make them accept these daily massacres.

With the simple logic of a child's mind I then saw it all in a flash, yet it took me twenty years to overcome the social convention upholding the eating of flesh, and to take the really consistent action of declining to consume any creature that has lived or felt.

Another revealing episode came later, early in my adult life. The scene was not a dark coal cellar, but a beautiful Cotswold manor house in spring. The lunch had just been laid on the table when the cat walked in with a mauled-looking object and laid it on the carpet before us. Consternation broke out in the family.

'How ghastly,' someone exclaimed. 'It's a baby bird she has killed and eaten the head off. Oh, what a horrible beast.'

Fury and indignation having been shown, and the cat having gone outside in disgrace, the matter of lunch again became uppermost.

'Oh Ruth dear,' said the hostess spontaneously, 'would you mind getting the lamb out of the larder?' As I carried it in, and the family sat down to enjoy their repast of politely cut slices taken from its flesh, I suddenly realized how incongruous it was. Here we were, furious with the cat for taking the head off a tiny bird, but someone had cut the throat of a lamb on our behalf so that we too might devour it in our more sophisticated fashion with knife and fork.

There are others who fully recognize the fact that they are eating animals, but feeling a little self-conscious and guilty, justify their action by announcing that the animals gain greatly in the spiritual sense by being physically consumed by man and contributing, as it were, to the maintenance of his life on earth.

In actual fact, of course, it is not at all necessary for man to eat meat to live. It is purely a matter of personal choice. Vegetarians are certainly no less healthy, and mostly a good deal more healthy, than meat-eaters. Not even those who are ill with such deficiency diseases as anaemia are prescribed liver in these modern times; the missing component is given in the far more direct and easily assimilated form of Vitamin B 12 tablets. In fact, in the world as a whole, far more people are vegetarians than meat-eaters; the necessity of eating meat is an idea belonging to our Western civilization.

That there can be any spiritual advantage for the animal in being used for slaughter is hardly a tenable theory, for it has no choice in the matter. This is quite different from the case of a dog motivated by personal devotion to give his life for his master. Those who have been in slaughterhouses will tell you how most animals have to be dragged on to the killing floor in a state of violent protest and terror.

Carrying the theory of spiritual uplift by physical consumption through to its logical conclusion, everyone should hope to be kidnapped by some great spiritual leader and served up as brunch for Billy Graham or supper for St Teresa of Avila, according to the branch of spiritual advancement we adhere to; in fact we should be back to cannibalism.

The orthodox Christian will often shelve the whole question of eating animals by saying that Jesus ate meat and he did not directly oppose the killing of animals. In fact, when he instituted Holy Communion, using the earthly forms of bread and wine as its vehicles, he at once wiped out animal sacrifice for religious purposes. That, at least, was a vast step forward; and did He not say, 'You have many things to learn but you cannot bear them now.' Was this possibly a forecast of new demands on our thinking; an extension of the spiritual path we, coming later, are meant to follow. The clue we have to the path in the objective picture of the final state is when 'The lion shall lie down with the lamb.'

How can we expect animals to give up killing while man—who breeds millions of animals each year purely for food—is the greatest killer of them all.

Our friendship with Mrs Leonard caused me to consider this problem of animals a stage further and to study the problem of what became of them after death. She had herself had some strange experiences relating to this question, and had come to hold a very definite opinion. The first revelation came to her in an out-of-the-body experience one night. She wrote of it in her book *My Life in Two Worlds*.

One night I found myself leaving the physical body, but instead of the soaring upward motion, I had a heavy weighted feeling, as if I were forced to travel in a horizontal position, and suddenly found myself in a narrow, dark street. I found I could just stand upright now, as if I were adjusting myself more easily to the atmosphere, but I did not want to put my feet on the ground as it was covered with mud and slime. Gloomy buildings, like stables, huddled against each other so closely that they almost touched, leaving only sufficient room for one to walk between. Here and there I saw a wider opening, which appeared to lead into a kind of yard, into which the doors of some of the stables opened. I looked in and saw that the yard was crowded with animals—bullocks, pigs and sheep—dead, and yet alive. I *knew* they were dead, but I could also see that they were alive, too. They moved very slightly, many lay on the ground. I understood at once from their appearance that they had just been slaughtered.

I pulled myself together with a tremendous effort. The place and everything in it was so horrible that I did indeed have to make an effort—a great one. I noticed that there was a great difference in the substance of this plane, compared with that of the planes where I had seen ordinary discarnate human life. Even the suicides' plane was different, inasmuch as it seemed fixed and solid. *This* dreadful place gave me the impression that it had but *temporary* existence. I will not go into more details of the place and the condition of the animals, but only tell you that it was indeed most dreadful and repulsive in every possible sense.

I soon became aware that somebody was speaking to me, somebody whom I could not see, and who seemed to be a long way off. This person, who I afterwards found out was one of my spiritual Guides, told me that the place lay *between* the earth and etheric planes. Its misery was due to the tremendous slaughtering of animals for food that takes place daily; so much strong animal life is *suddenly* forced out of the actual physical condition into one that is very close indeed to earth, and yet is in no way part of the spiritual world. What happens to the animal astrals I do not know. I was only shown this horrible scene on the astral side, which followed all the killing and pain on the earth side. In the very air around me was a most definite feeling of terrible fear, suffering, and blind resentment that was even more tangible than the buildings and walls. My Guide told me that it was this awful *feeling* that was to be deplored, not only because it was an indication of the sufferings that these wretched animals had experienced, but because it affected the spiritual and mental atmosphere of the earth, and had a bad effect on human life and progress.

Now, up to a short time ago I had been a flesh-eater. Every day I had my cutlet, cut off the joint, or piece of chicken. It always looked so nice and appetizing that somehow one hadn't thought of it as being a piece of something that had walked and breathed, and felt pain and discomfort, just as we do ourselves. From time to time Feda had tried to discourage me and other people, too, from eating meat, but as there is only a limited amount of power that can be used, I had been obliged to devote it to the needs of bereaved sitters, and so had little opportunity of questioning Feda on this point. Now, after all I had seen, and the explanation given me of the reason for the existence of this horrible plane, I felt I wanted to ask several questions, so I got one or two sitters to ask Feda about it, while they were talking to her through me.

One thing we asked was, 'What would happen if we all suddenly stopped eating meat? Surely, the world would be overrun with cattle, sheep and other animals?'

'No,' said Feda. 'You wouldn't be overrun with them because you would stop breeding them. There would not be anything like the number you have got if you hadn't purposely encouraged them by breeding them.'

She said that, in time, as people understood more of the Spiritual World, they would eat less flesh, and be better for it, and from my own more recent personal experience, I have come to the definite conclusion that Feda was right. Since I gave up meat entirely a few years ago, my health has improved very much, in spite of strenuous work done under sometimes very difficult conditions. My husband, too, has found great benefit through becoming a vegetarian, and the same has been told us by many of our friends. My mind is clearer, and I am more 'open' to direct spiritual guidance than I used to be.

You must not think that all animals that die, or have to be 'put to sleep', go to such places as I have described. An animal that you have loved and who has loved you, whether it be horse, dog, cat, or bird, goes usually to the third sphere where somebody takes care of it, and where it leads a normal animal life (except that it doesn't reproduce its species as it would on earth), and is even brought to see you at times while you are still on earth. I know you will meet your pets, the animal companions that you have loved. I have seen my special cats, and also a dog, a pekinese, to whom my husband and I were very much attached. It seems as if the animals who love, and are loved, attain to spiritual rights and have an after-life in the spiritual world, just as we do. Whether their 'post-physical' lives continue for ever, I do not know. I rather doubt it; that is, I doubt if they continue everlastingly in animal form, but they certainly live for a considerable time in the shape we loved and knew them by, and, thank goodness, they will live with us again when we pass over.

There is considerable evidence that animals do not 'die' when they are killed, and this important fact should be widely realized. The figures issued by the R.S.P.C.A. of the number of healthy animals which they are asked to put to sleep—in many cases, just because the owners have lost interest in them—is astounding. A French friend, who had been observing life in England, remarked one day suddenly, 'It is a good thing that you have not legalized euthanasia in this country or people would be rushing off all the time putting their grandmothers and old aunts away judging by the rate they keep on having their animals put to sleep.'

Of course it is better to do this with animals than abandon them, or leave them in a bad home, but since death is not the end there are many associated problems that must be taken into consideration. The important thing is that they should get away from the earth in a reasonable time and be taken care of by those whom Mrs Leonard mentions in her book who are specially occupied in this kind of work, even as they are here. Of course, where someone who loved them already has gone over, then it is easy, but it is important to link them in thought, telling the person that the animal has died. When someone living alone dies, leaving a devoted animal, it is probably far kinder to have it put to sleep. If possible this should be done not too soon after their passing, as a friend's story seems to show.

She attended the funeral service at a crematorium for an old man she knew. During the service she saw a little brown dog running about the chapel, and thought it had got in by mistake. As the doors into the inner part of the crematorium opened at the appropriate moment and the coffin glided through, she saw the little dog jump on top of it. She was horrified and called out, 'Stop that dog!' and then suddenly realized that the dog had vanished.

She later learnt that the old man had owned just such a brown dog.

How far an animal, though in its after-life body, could be linked with this earth until his owner's physical remains are put away is not clear. It could not possibly experience the physical pain, but it might experience the mental pain and terror in following its owner to cremation. This must remain an open question. It is one important for consideration, and perhaps those who leave instructions for their animals to be put to sleep when they die should stipulate that this should not be done until after their funeral.

There are, of course, many examples of animals returning to earth on happier occasions, simply because they loved their homes or because someone from the Other Side brings them. This has occurred in mine many times. The first was when I was upstairs in the bathroom, and I saw a small brown cat walking across the floor. It was so real it never struck me as anything abnormal. Thinking that my little tabby cat, Pussy Pockets, had followed me from downstairs, I bent to pick her up. As I did so I noticed a curious thing: her right hindleg seemed to have faded rather from sight, although she still stood upright, as if on four legs. By the time my hands reached her level and I brought them together to gather her up, I realized that I was only grasping thin air. There was no cat there.

We then had our two old friends Mr and Mrs Roberts living

in the house prior to getting their own home. I had known them all their lives and can vouch for their great integrity. It was Mr Roberts who had driven our car at the vicarage. I went downstairs and stood in the hall talking to Mrs Roberts about something quite unconnected. As I did so, I saw her turn, while her eyes followed something across the floor which I could not see.

'Did you see a cat that was not really there?' I asked.

'Yes,' she replied.

Then her husband called through the door from the dining-room, 'Yes, I have seen that cat too.'

In a later sitting with my mother she alluded to this episode and said that she wanted me to know that, when the cat appeared, she was there too, but it was much easier to materialize a cat than a human as they were in a sense closer to nature. The cat she had brought was Dodie, a tiny brown one we brought back after we had lived in the Lake District. My mother had chosen Dodie because she had been so thin and delicate while on earth. She never recovered from her harsh life on a farm. Now, in the after-life, she had altered so much for the better.

There was then a gap of some years before the cats reappeared. A medium who came to stay, and who used my bedroom, said the room was full of power, and that cats kept jumping on and off her bed during the night. It was not until Mrs Beresford, who seems to have natural psychic power, became my tenant in the flat upstairs that we began to obtain evidence of individual cats appearing again. Her cat encountered one when crossing the bedroom floor, as was shown by its strange antagonistic behaviour towards something unseen. Then an invisible cat began to jump on her bed at night. She described its habit of circling round several times before it settled, and then plumping down into a sort of 'nest' created by its actions on the bed. This was a particular habit of Charlie, a tabby cat, much resembling Mrs Beresford's cat, Smoky, who had died a year or two before Mrs Beresford moved in.

On several occasion I also experienced a cat jumping on my bed. It was especially interesting one night when twice I felt the bedclothes being pulled down, in exactly the same way as Pussy Pockets and a black cat of mine had used to do it when they grew old; both would pull themselves up on to the bed instead of jumping (and both had by then passed into the After Life). Next morning Mrs Beresford, knowing nothing of this episode, came downstairs and remarked, 'I had two of your pussies on my bed last night!'

There was corroboration also from other sources. The apparitions were not only seen by Mrs Beresford and me, who being interested in the problem of appearances from the Unseen might be considered gullible or motivated by wishful thinking. In an annexe to my house there lived a Mr Hocquard, a man who had himself been brought up as a member of the religious sect called The Brethren, and was always taught that anything to do with the supernatural savoured of the Devil. I have seldom talked to him about our communications or psychic experiences, and he has certainly never wished to join in them in any way. An episode some weeks after Koo, the older of the two black cats, passed on, therefore caused us some amazement.

I usually shut Oliver, my other black cat, up on his own in my sitting-room whenever Smoky comes down from Mrs Beresford's flat for his daily run, for they don't get on. One day I had done this when John Hocquard came in to see me about something, absent-mindedly leaving the sitting-room door open. 'Shut the door,' I said, 'or Oliver will be out and there may be a fight.'

'Don't be silly,' he replied. 'You are over fussy about them. Oliver is in the hall now and there is no fighting.'

'But Oliver is fast asleep on the hearthrug,' I replied. 'Look.' And there he was. 'He's been there a whole hour.'

'But a black cat met me at the front door as I came in.'

'Why, you must have seen Koo,' I exclaimed. 'He always met me at the front door.'

On another occasion Mr Hocquard, trying this time to be careful about the danger of fights, went upstairs and knocked on Mrs Beresford's flat door, calling out urgently:

'Hi, you have let your cat out. He is on the stairs.' Mrs Beresford investigated matters and found Smoky safely esconced in the flat. It was evidently Charlie he had mistaken for Smoky, as the two had similar tabby markings. He must have materialized very clearly to take Mr Hocquard in so completely.

I must explain that there cannot be any possible chance of a neighbour's cat coming in and causing confusion. The garden is fenced round by high wire-netting to prevent my cats getting out or others coming in. There can therefore be no normal explanation. The only tenable one seems to be that those we have loved in the cat world are still alive after death, just as our human friends are, and that they like to come back and visit us. In the case of Dodie he was brought back by a human wishing to make the presence of visitors from the Unseen known.

Speaking about animals in the After Life, Feda said that my father 'was so glad to say that animals had a better life on the Other Side than on earth, much better, they are not exploited there'. He had quite a lot of birds in his garden, which he loves, not in cages but free, she explained, 'and the birds there will sit on the dogs' heads, they are not frightened of one another, the dogs don't eat the cats and the cats don't eat the birds, they all live in a friendly manner together'. 'Daddy says,' Feda went on, 'what struck him so forcibly was the absolute harmony here, the sense of brotherhood there is over there.'

Animals are therefore all part of God's scheme of survival—'Not one sparrow shall fall.' Our responsibility towards them is inescapable.

9

Unseen help in working out the pattern of life

In the present chapter it will be necessary to write more of events in my own personal life and the messages received about them, not because I wish to be egotistical and assume that there was anything unique about them, but because I want to show how there is a pattern and purpose in one's life as an individual, and in my own I can now look back and see how it was gradually being worked out with the help of those we loved on the Other Side, and how we were brought to accept vast changes in our environment so as to fulfil this. These were changes that we would never have been ready to accept had we not had this help and enlightenment from our unseen friends. By postponing them we might have frustrated the plan for my life and put off doing things I was meant to do for God.

It is far too much the fashion, even among some who have knowledge of the Unseen, to decry personal messages on practical matters as sentimental and childish; or even as dangerous, labelling them as coming from the lower spheres. I personally deplore this new kind of religious snobbery. Man is capable of living and communicating at several different levels, and from all of these he can gather experience and wisdom. Awareness of other states can never justify our ignoring the urgency of work to help people and improve conditions in this earthly world, helped (as in the case of our crippled friend's chair) by power from the Unseen. Illumination and co-operation with those in another life, who can see further than us, can if used rightly enable us to do this work better and more effectively. It is all a part of the 'Whole Life' which God has destined. It is the only kind of spiritual life which makes sense while avoiding an academic preoccupation with a luxurious form of soul culture.

This problem about the progress of my life seems to have

concerned Ralph from the first. Even in our initial sitting Feda remarked, 'He will protect and help his sister all he can.'

A year later Feda remarked:

> He has been helping Ruth, looking after her. He is not worried about her, but he would like her to know he does look after her. She has been doing rather well at something to do with books and he has been helping her. She was rather undecided, she could not get enough confidence about it, she has so much sometimes and then she loses it—that is where he comes in and helps her.

My mother has pencilled a note against this in the report, 'Ruth was writing a book, but the fact was quite unknown to us.'

This emphasis on the fact that he wanted me to know that he was helping me was highly evidential. It came as a great surprise to me personally, for the latter years had not been easy when he, being five years older, had grown into a man and gone on to university, while I remained a teenager at boarding school. By my own wish I had been sent to a large 'public school' as like my brother's as possible. Its system trained people for leadership and independence, and after a year or two there I absorbed the atmosphere and began to assert myself. My mother, who had been sent to a small private school where Victorian meekness was thought to be the chief virtue, could not appreciate this development.

But I did not go to boarding school until I was fifteen. Previously I had been rather sketchily educated with shared governesses, lessons from father and much encouragement in independent reading. My mother, whose childhood was made unhappy by fierce Victorian discipline, had used little on her own children. My brother, however, who had been to boarding school from nine years old and been nurtured on the classics before taking up medicine, had a great appreciation of order and discipline. He used to give my mother helpful advice over my upbringing. Secretly I admired this, but it was too much for me to accept it openly from a brother whom I looked on as my contemporary and equal. So I resisted his efforts to shape me into the kind of person he thought I should be and no doubt appeared obstinate and unruly.

To add to the difficulties my mother naturally adored my brother so much that it led to feelings of jealousy on my part. So many grown-ups admired his charm of manner and quiet thoughtfulness and wanted to see more of him, while I, a leggy teenager, received only a friendly greeting. When Ralph brought his medical-student friends home they talked of the university and the medical world and none asked me to join in their activities. His endless brotherly teasing, which had formerly irked me so much, though it at least made me feel that he was aware of my presence, ceased, but I found his calm poise and detachment far harder to bear.

These were, of course, only growing pains. Had he lived we should have left them behind. Knowing Ralph's true calibre I cannot imagine him ever neglecting any member of the family who really needed his help. But since he passed at a time when we had temporarily grown apart, I never imagined the gulf being bridged, even though divided by the wider gulf of death. It was typical of his conscientiousness and capability that he made a special point of compensating for my omission

Communication liberated us from the shadow of my mother's preoccupation with her grief, as I have already shown. However, regarding our physical surroundings we became more attached to them than we had been before in the realization of Ralph's constant presence. After we bought the Vicarage we enlarged the house to our own taste and kept Ralph's room exactly as he had left it. I was as keen as my parents to remain. I had known only the one home, and now I was old enough for a social life I had made many friends and wanted to keep them.

It is therefore indicative of a mind and purpose independent of ours that, tracing the records of these early years, one perceives a quiet purpose in the redressing of brotherly indifference and a systematic effort to acclimatize us to the idea that we must move to London so that I should undertake work for which I was intended.

A few months before my father passed, Ralph expressed a longing that we might be more in the centre of activity. He spoke of a new band of people with scientific minds—friends of

Jim's who had formed a circle in London and who might produce some interesting results.

'We should have liked you to be in it. I wish you lived nearer London,' Ralph remarked, 'so that you could go to these things.'

We agreed with this regret, but accepted the position as inevitable. It never entered our heads that any permanent change would come about.

I had always felt strongly that I had a vocation of some kind in life, and that I was not meant to lead a life of mere social enjoyment. Ever since early childhood I had felt the deep urge and conviction to write. I had started my first novel, a historical one, at the age of five. Unfortunately, as I grew older, the inevitable self-consciousness of adolescence crept in and spoilt the spontaneous flow. The fear of failure disturbed me, and certain amateur attempts at publication being unsuccessful, my enthusiasm for this kind of self-expression was considerably blunted. As Ralph so truly said in allusion to the novel I was writing secretly, 'Ruth cannot get enough confidence about the thing she is writing, she has so much sometimes and then she loses it.'

10

Exodus

At a sitting about nine months later, Feda suddenly came out with a loud exclamation, 'Exodus!' Then she went on to say:

> What is Ralph saying about an exodus? Is he helping you to make some plans, not immediate? They want you to talk them over quietly for they feel there will be new developments and openings, new plans to be made that are partly through Ruth. He is very pleased about all this for he has got a very strong feeling about this and when he is very pleased you can feel it bubbling out. It is not what he says, he is pleased without saying it. He was going over and saying 'Bless you my child' wasn't he naughty? He says it is his *hall mark* of approval.

This was most evidential as he often called me 'The child', and my father referred to me as 'That child' constantly. Feda then said, 'I cannot make out whether Ralph is being serious, not when he does these things.' This was also evidential, for much of Ralph's humour was put over in a mock seriousness that someone like Feda, who had never lived in England, might not at first recognize. It was typical of him to use these words and speak in this manner.

> New things are opening out and he wants her to fit in with them. He just wants her to be her natural self. He does not want her to be anxious and feel will she fit in with them. He knows it will work out all right.

About a year later Feda said quite spontaneously during our sitting:

> Ralph has got an impression that a good many new people are going to be important to Ruth, new ones altogether. He

has got a feeling that Ruth is not going to have an ordinary life, she is going to have what he thinks is an interesting life.

My mother asked, 'Is it going to be away from her present home?' and Ralph replied:

He cannot quite tell that yet but it may have to be. If so, he will try and arrange things so that you are not too much parted. He was talking it over with his father and he is saying they feel that it does not matter if you yourself work in one place more than another. They do not want you to have to live where you are. If by doing work in another place it would enable you to be with Ruth it would be better for you to go, but they are leaving it all rather vague for the present as they do not want to determine it all. Don't feel tied to conditions because there is work for you to do and it might be difficult for you to do as much as you want to there. Besides things are not the same since he passed, they have brought innovations and he wanted you to feel just a little bit inclined for changes. He wants you to take up the problem and work it out on the happiest lines possible.

He did not want you to think because you felt a little better that you should go on interminably with the old routine. He was trying to say 'Go ahead, go ahead, don't say perhaps we ought not to be doing this, my conscience is uneasy and so and so.'

He is very pleased indeed with plans now and he says I have got something serious to say about them.

Oh [Feda said], Daddy wants to say something, because I saw him dodging about. Ralph is standing here by my knees and Daddy is behind Ralph. I always know when I see him dodging about that he wants to say something.

The plans you are making are not being made simply and entirely because you want a change and a rest, there is something else at the back of them, prompting you to make them.

In answer to a direct question from my mother, Ralph said:

He is happy about Ruth. She has got to get her experience

through people and things that may be rather different to people and things of the past. Things will work out for her right and you have to keep her and yet let her go as if on a piece of elastic. By letting her go you will keep her. She is going to be in touch with rather different people from those you and Daddy used to know, even different to the people you and Daddy used to like. It may seem very different but it has to be, because Ruth has got to get experience for what she has to do later in different ways to you and Daddy. But Ruth and you will never be separated. She will always be on a piece of elastic like stockings.

In answer to my mother's direct question, 'Have you any idea what work Ruth will take up?' father replied:

Don't try and arrange anything at present. Leave things open as far as you can, as long as you can, because I asked Feda to tell you that I thought things would move very quickly and suddenly once they began to move. I am sure that things will open out very much after you get to London. It will make a great difference to you. I am not sure whether you will like it at first but it will lead to things, interesting things and quite unique because you know Ralph told you you would be doing some work for them. He wants you to feel it might be coming sooner than they at first thought. He says he feels your move will coincide with the new work and will take you into it.

Here my mother asked if it was psychic work, and he replied that it was.

It will be very interesting you see and you will like it, only he knows what an uprooting it is, but it is right to do it. You are going to be taken into a new sphere of *activity* [stressed in the direct voice]. You will be brought into touch with people who will be important to you for work. This will concern Ruth and be for the happiness of you both. Happiness will come out of it because you are definitely doing something with them and for them. He feels you are going to be connected with some special branch of spiritual and psychic

> work. Don't try to define it beforehand just come south and be ready for it.

In those days the words 'psychic' and 'spiritual' were seldom linked. The only societies in existence were designated as either 'spiritualistic' or 'psychic'. My father was extremely keen for the Church to alter its point of view on these things. and bring them more together. He had even begun to draft a letter to the Archbishop of Canterbury on the subject, but his illness cut his efforts short. As far as I can recall he never actually envisaged a society. It was a good many years before the Churches' Fellowship for Psychic and Spiritual Studies was founded to bring people together in the study of these two, previously alienated, subjects—a movement to which I have belonged for some years. It therefore appears that the following statement by him was a definite piece of clairvoyance:

> I have learnt, Daddy says, since I came to the spirit side that when one reaches a certain stage in one's development or earth experience when one has reached a certain point spiritually and mentally things do happen in that way. Now I feel we as a family march together so much in line and things happen in such a way that what happens to one happens to all.
>
> So they will be with you, working with you and taking care of you and bringing the right conditions round you and the right people.

Much of this message is easily interpreted in after years. The statement that the plans we had made were not only because mother wanted a change and rest proved so true. The work we did was to be closely linked with international events, then, as it were, gathering about us unseen, and none of that or our psychic work could have been done had we never come to London.

The reference to my meeting very different people from those my parents had known also proved very accurate. We had not evidently at the time made up our minds that I was to go to the London School of Economics, for mother put a direct question to my father regarding what I should do in London, and he merely replied: 'Things will open out there.'

Actually, I enrolled in the London School of Economics that October for a social science course. There, for the first time in my life, I met intellectual atheists and members of the Communist Party. This was what Ralph meant when he said: 'Ruth will be in touch with rather different people from those you and Daddy used to know, different to the people you used to like.' The whole of my faith and general outlook had never before been so strongly challenged. I had to begin thinking all over again, and for a while became very depressed and puzzled until I could accept these very different points of view and work out my own faith in relation to them.

The fact that we should not like London at first was also very true in another sense. We found ourselves plunged into all the vast problems of poverty and the slums in a big city during a severe economic slump. This, and the initial strangeness of living in such a vast city with only a limited circle of friends, made us feel at times very overwhelmed and lonely. But the promise of interesting and unique things has been proved only too true when I look back over my subsequent life.

I became very depressed and developed a bad throat, so, in the spring, we left London and spent six months or so at my uncle's house in the Midlands so that I could recover from a tonsil operation. But in spite of our long absence from London the idea of a home there was definitely accepted, evidently because father and Ralph spoke about it in the sitting.

> Daddy says all you are trying to do and all you are doing is right, only things are coming in that are difficult. Have you been held up by someone not being well? I get a feeling of illness at the back of you not to do with Ruth.

My mother has made a note on the records here: 'Yes, my brother had been ill.' So this has a double meaning.

> Ralph says you were trying to lift the burden but you got so very tired. It is wonderful when you have been flattened out how you have come up again.

A year later we seem to have grown quite used to the fact that we should live in London permanently, for father said, speaking direct to my mother:

> Did Feda tell you that we thought your headquarters would be in London? It will be a very good thing too. It is far better for you now we are over here. You get into touch with interesting people you know. It is not such a heavy life either. I was afraid that you might simply become ill, and not come over to me but go on lingering if you stayed where you were, the very thing we wanted to avoid.

It is interesting to find how one can frustrate or co-operate with a plan to preserve physical health for, apparently, a longer period during life on earth. The same concern for our physical health was shown in our next sitting a year later, when Ralph gave quite a long and detailed review of some trouble in my back and mentioned that he had given it an examination, though I was unaware of the fact.

> You know I have been with you impressing you in various ways. He has been helping Ruth a great deal. Don't you think he is getting hold of her health better, because he is especially helping her in various ways. He thinks he has done her good. Her back is getting stronger. She still has to rest. He always impresses her to lie flat on it. He also tries to impress her when she is lying on her back to try to think she is spreading her back out sideways, especially from the armpits outward. He does not want her to narrow her back and lie on it all squirmed up. He wants her to expand it. What Ruth wants is relaxation all down the spine. She is rather tense down the spine.

When my mother suggested a further visit to our osteopath, Ralph asked:

> Did not he find the bit that was out? Well there was a bit just near her shoulders that was out, and above it, rather between the shoulders, one above the other. Then there was

also something wanted adjusting down here that was bad for her. I suppose he [the osteopath] thinks he has got them in again, but there is a slight slipping.

You know the spine, Ralph says, or anything connected with it is something we are very sensitive to on our side. The spine, the solar plexus and the brain, those parts are so much connected, they are all one. Some people almost think there. Ruth almost thinks internally, that's why she gets upset inside. We sense these things more than we should anything like a leg or an arm.

In the spring, just before I completed my social science course, the sitting opened with the statement that they were very happy about my work. Things were going to turn out all right. There were going to be some difficult patches, they added warningly.

We are helping to guide things on to the right lines, but don't look too far ahead and don't weigh things up too much just now. He spoke of a move. It is a change to do with Ruth it is happy but it will lose its importance in view of the importance of what has caused it.

Twice in earlier years Ralph had warned me of a setback that would occur in my work, and which I was not to be upset by, for without it I might have overlooked something more important. 'Our family seems to be cut out for rather funny and unexpected things to happen.'

He then spoke of not letting myself become depressed by mere physical years (since I was rather older than most of my fellow students). 'Physically a few years don't matter,' he said, 'but being conscious of them does.'

Ralph then continued:

On this side of life I see that the whole earth is run on magnetism and power of attraction. It is called polar activity and if you keep your positive pole working things will be all right. But [he added] Ruth has got to be quietly sure of herself. Sometimes Ruth has been disappointed at her share in the work she is doing and wondered is it quite worthwhile. At present under present conditions this is the right place for her because it is out of these conditions that Ruth will find her right path, just step by step. Things will happen to Ruth in such a queer unexpected way. It will work out right but there is a good deal of work to be done before it can. Don't regret anything or say, 'Oh, I wish it had happened so and so.' Let things work out normally and they will be all right for her.

Looking back I realize that this rather nebulous communication covered so many unexpected events that lay in the near future and which I was to come to.

That summer brought success. I passed my examination at the London School of Economics and obtained my Social Science Certificate—one of the things that Ralph was happy about, I presume. As for finding my right path step by step and unexpectedly, this came very true.

I decided I would now like to do some specialized training and try to become a medical social worker. I was sent to work at two different hospitals.

The departmental head in the first was a most interesting person, with whom I had everything in common. She praised my work very much and appreciated rather than criticized what I had learnt previously from helping people in our parish work at home. Later, though well on in middle age, she was to join the Steiner movement and leave the profession to teach mentally retarded children. She was an exceptional person in many ways and had never let herself fall into an institutional groove.

The head at the other hospital was the exact opposite. She was the typical dictator so often found in an institution, her mainsprings dominance over others and organization. This led her into collisions with all kinds of staff members, not only her students. She was not on speaking terms with the medical superintendent. She told me with, I thought, some pride that she had told him if he wished to say anything to her he must put it in writing.

It was an interesting experience to encounter these two different types of women and it made me aware of the sharp distinction between the institutional woman and the woman at home. 'You can never have an official manner,' the fierce one said deprecatingly, explaining in a few curt sentences (when we happened to meet in the ladies' room) that she would be writing a letter to the authorities *not* recommending me for her profession, thereby terminating my career as a hospital social worker. As she went out and slammed the door, I felt thankful that, if that was what an official manner was like, at least I had not got one.

Now I began to understand what Ralph had meant when he said:

> It is out of these conditions that Ruth will find her right path, just step by step. Things will happen in such *queer unexpected ways. Don't regret anything* or say I wish it had happened so and so. Things will work out right but there is a good deal of work to be done before they can.

Were the paths of other people's lives really to be so easily and accurately charted? Looking at the problem from a viewpoint that saw both worlds it seemed different. Would the treatment necessarily be the right thing for them? Were they, in fact, destined to remain on this earth?

Even our fierce chief had been silenced by the problem of one patient who entered her office one day. He was a middle-aged man who should normally have been in the full vigour of his life. But his voice was only a husky whisper, owing to a chronically tubercular larynx. The doctor had recommended that he should come back into hospital. 'I am not going in again,' he said. 'It won't do me any permanent good now. My wife and family will be much better off when I am dead than hanging on with me in this state. She can make definite plans then to take a post where she can have the child and really get her life going again.'

The fierce one looked at him.

'I think you are behaving like the ostrich,' she said, 'but I admire you.'

After the door had shut on this urban Captain Oates, she was silent for a while as if even her cast-iron code of behaviour had been a little put out of line by the man's individualistic sincerity.

At the sitting after my hospital work had terminated, Feda said:

> Ralph has been with you a lot because there have been perplexing times to do with other people. We will patch it up. Don't plan too far ahead until you have got to, don't make plans so that you cannot break them because this is a time of changes and alterations. He does not want you to set the future in too strongly even in thought. Leave it because things are opening out and he wants them to open out connected with Ruth. You know he wanted this, but he did not want them to open out too soon. He sees them coming nearer but everything is not yet certain, things have got to form into line. The biggest thing cannot happen until other things have worked up a bit each side. All things work together for good if we let them but we usually put a spoke in the wheel by precipitating something that brings them into the wrong focus, the wrong position as regards ourselves.

Later, when he took control, father remarked that 'Ruth's work will get more and more interesting'. This came so true, and later I understood why fate had so to speak ejected me from the conventional institutional life, there being something far more suitable waiting round the corner.

In some ways I was a conventionalist. I had chosen a conventional school which reinforced my ideas and habits in its environment and led me to seek a conventional professor. But I had not yet come to recognize another part of myself which was to realize a diversity of interests in quite new and original fields as well as a capacity to excel far more among the people found in them, once I was free of the, to me, completely inhibiting conventional dictators. So I cannot but be grateful for the forces which took the matter out of my hands and placed me on the right road, even though it sometimes had to be through unpleasant experiences.

11

Widening horizons

The 'opening out' that Ralph saw for us was a very new and unexpected kind, entirely foreign to any previous trends in my thought and interest. But, like our move to London, it was very much part of the intended plan for my future work. So we had to be made used to the idea gradually.

The links leading to this new path had really started some years before, seeming to come about through some apparently indirect and chance contacts. A boy friend of mine, who worked in our neighbourhood in the north, had invited me to his home in the south for Whitsun. I realized that it lay close to a childhood friend, Irene, whom I had not seen for many years owing to the considerable distance. I therefore arranged to take this opportunity to visit her home after Whitsun while I was still in those parts.

As time went on, however, and the Whitsun visit drew nearer, I became rather worried about it, for I was aware that the young man admired me a good deal and my friends substantiated my impression. As I was not in love with him I did not want him to think that, through making this formal visit to his parents, I was prepared to marry him. In those days there was far more formality than there is today. I therefore began seriously to contemplate cancelling both visits, for I could not visit the neighbourhood and ignore the young man's invitation.

We happened to have a sitting at that time, and without my even mentioning the matter, Feda broke in unexpectedly with the question:

> Have you had an invitation to go and stay somewhere? Well, you should accept it because it may be important it may lead to something.

When advice comes through quite spontaneously like this I always take note of it. So I decided not to cancel my visits to the south but to let events run their course. When the time came, as so often happens to me, they took a quite unexpected turn. I was stricken just before Whitsun with a really bad cold, not a slight one which could have left me undecided as to whether or not to travel. I could only retire to bed, and once I was better the Whitsun holiday was over. The young man had returned to his job in our neighbourhood, so there was no occasion for me to visit his home. There was, however, just time to pay a visit to my other friend, Irene. Through her family there came a link that was to change my whole life.

It seems as if our contacts on the Other Side of Life were always working to widen our horizons as part of an intended plan. It is like the strand of a particular colour woven through a total design. My friend's father was a north country business-man, and while the family had retained the warmth and friendliness of the north, they had become very prosperous since going south and had gained a wide experience in many aspects of earthly life, especially foreign travel.

My mother, who always left for a holiday very tired, had a great wish to take a cruise to the Norwegian fjords, having heard it was such a relaxing way to see the scenery. 'Norway,' I remarked deprecatingly, when first she broached the subject in earlier years to me alone. 'Don't let's go to a grey country like that and so far away.'

So for the moment the matter had been dropped. My psychic intuition was certainly not working then. Little did I know what this country would come to mean to me. I was not ready to accept, as Ralph said, that 'Things have to work out and come together for new developments for you'.

In those early days I must have been one of the most insular people imaginable. The only foreigners I had ever seen were the foreign governesses who came to teach our squire's daughter. They seemed very unhappy and temperamental, and when they were apologized for by people saying, 'Oh well, you see, dear, they are foreign,' it made me feel even more prejudiced towards people in other countries.

We did once take a trip to France soon after my father died.

It was intended to be a complete change for mother after the strain she had been through. His sister, my favourite aunt, wanted us to go and see the country where our family originated. The trip was not at all a success. I felt quite unsympathetic to the people and surroundings. I was upset by many things, including the starving quayside cats, about which I could do nothing as there was no French equivalent of the R.S.P.C.A. to call in. And there were many other things in this entirely different country's way of life in which I felt unable to participate: so I became frustrated and unhappy. The only pleasant things I carried away were a vivid impression of the walls of the old town of St Malo (later, alas, damaged so badly during the Second World War), a memory of the intense blue of the sea off the northern coast of France and a set of beautiful lace table mats which I have still. So on the whole I had after this an antipathy to foreign travel.

Once they had begun, my visits to Irene and her family continued, my mother often accompanying me. On one of these, being especially tired after a heavy year's work in London, my mother again broached the subject of a cruise to Norway and asked our friends about it. She found by a strange coincidence that they hoped to go to Norway too. With their support as expert travellers, we found ourselves booking on an English cruise ship in no time and setting off for this unknown land.

I shall never forget my first glimpse of that country which I had tried so hard to avoid. As we sailed up the coast I had expected us to be overshadowed at once by dark dramatic mountains. With some amazement, therefore, I found myself gazing through a porthole at tiny strips of land scarcely visible in the grey light. These were the outer islands which I was to come to know so well as the heralds of that fantastic land.

Feeling a little unsteady after the crossing, I blinked at them unbelievingly. They looked like wraiths from Viking times as they lined the horizon, disappearing now and then from view into the restless grey waters.

Later, as the rocky landmarks came nearer, they took on a far more realistic appearance. There were small stocky buildings and beacons like tiny white dustbins with perpetually winking eyes in the lids.

As we drew closer to shore the waters took on the smoothness of dark marble. The islands were formed of less sheer rocks and were sites for immaculate, painted cottages set in tiny creeks where boats were moored. Here and there families could be seen sitting on small green patches of grass.

Visiting a country by a cruise ship from one's own land is not the ideal way to assimilate it. One can remain so entirely British except for the few hours spent on shore, usually devoted to some organized expedition. But, in spite of this drawback, I fell in love with Norway from the moment I first set foot on its soil. I cannot explain why any more than one can explain why one falls in love with a particular individual. But, like a happy marriage, I have never found cause to seek divorce.

I do not wish to dogmatize and prove irrevocably that Norway is the finest country in the world. Norway is human, and therefore, besides its many unique gifts, it has its faults. But the important thing for me was that I had learnt to love a country despite its faults. Brought up at home on the remnants of an ideal of a powerful Empire—a brittle image which most of my generation had thrown away—my deep affection for Norway, with its characteristics of simplicity and solid integrity, came as a great delight and made a vast change in my views.

It also completely changed my attitude to other countries and 'foreigners', providing the gateway to all my subsequent international work by opening out a vast new horizon.

Even so, no country has ever filled the place in my heart that Norway has. This may be due to the great personal warmth and hospitality of her people, which I have experienced literally in hundreds of homes, or it may be her forthright honesty in contrast to smooth expediency of the great powers in foreign affairs. But I feel that there is some even greater link and one which goes back into the distant past. Perhaps I was a Norwegian in another life, but that is only a personal opinion and another story.

Subsequently we went to Norway each year, no dislike of foreign travel or grey weather henceforward deterring us. Luckily my mother shared the love I felt for the country. We went alone the next year, and on an entirely Norwegian boat, *The Meteor*, which was going right up the coast to the North

Cape. It had in fact been the Kaiser's yacht, which the British had captured in the First World War and sold to the Norwegians. Passing out of the dark customs shed we suddenly saw her exquisite prow, picked out in white and gold, protruding above us into the industrial severity of Tyneside. It must have been late, for the deck lights were on and the band was playing ready for dinner. Like Alice through the looking glass, we stepped into an unknown fairyland.

The impact of northern Norway is something that must be experienced personally; the gradual drawing out of the northern night and the almost vibrant gleam of greens and golds as they mingle at night on the deep waters can never be adequately described. The strange shape of dark rocks, silhouetted age-old against the glowing skyline, are untouched by civilization. Further north the almost burdensome, perpetual sun spares few moments for sleep and relaxation, even in twilight. The sun is brightest at 3 a.m., with dazzling blue lights on the glacier and the fields of golden buttercups on the lower mountain slopes. Truly, we thought, we had glimpsed the Elysian fields, and my mother and I said to each other, 'This must be like heaven really is.'

It was significant that, years later, in a sitting with my mother shortly after her passing, the medium said:

> Your mother tells me that she had a home from which you could see beautiful sunsets, and she was very fond of going out and looking at them [which was quite correct]. She wants me to say that over here the colours are wonderful but not the same. You have, however, seen something on earth that resembles them. She is showing me a mountainous country that you used to visit where there were wonderful blue lights on the mountains you used to be enthralled by. She wants me to say that the colours over here remind her exactly of those.

I had to think about this for a short while, for Norway was not the only mountainous country we had been to. Then it came to me unmistakably that it was on seeing the blue on the Svartisen glacier at 3 a.m. on our unforgettable trips to the north that we had discussed this matter.

Away in England, Ralph was keeping in touch even while we were on our cruise. He spoke to Jim's mother at one sitting and said, 'Mummie is not well. But don't tell her. She will find out quite soon enough herself, but tell her the sofa has been used long enough.'

When my mother returned to England she found she had a small growth in her breast and entered hospital at once to have it removed. Jim's mother came to visit her forthwith, well briefed for the occasion and bearing Ralph's message.

Ralph's remarks regarding my mother's health were most appropriate. Had she discovered the lump while in the far north far from medical aid, she would have worried terribly. But since she did not know the cruise proved a splendid tonic and made her very fit for the operation, from which she rapidly recovered.

The reference to the sofa was also evidential, as my mother had been letting a lonely friend sleep on the one in the sitting-room. Although she was a very nice person and only came in at night, it was rather tiring for mother who always became so concerned for everybody and their problems.

After mother's operation my uncle took us to Stockholm for a change. It was not a very happy visit as the clouds of war were gathering. We landed there during the Munich crisis.

We had few Swedish friends and in the impersonal luxury of a vast hotel we felt lonely and apprehensive. *The Times*, England's essential pillar of international opinion and world news, always arrived a day late. We could not follow the news bulletins on the Swedish radio, and inquiries about the international situation from hoteliers or receptionists only evinced a flow of kindly but conditioned clichés, evidently acquired professionally to soothe the apprehensive customer.

My mother and I, who had no commitments at home, were not so alarmed by the possibility of being shut up in neutral Sweden for the duration of a war as was my uncle. He had his business to consider, his house and his official appointments. He became desperately anxious, practically imagining the Germans would arrive at the gates at any moment.

Things came to a head for us one particularly anxious night in the middle of our stay when my uncle became almost convinced that war was inevitable. The Swedish Air Force, as if to divert our minds from the grim reality of its *raison d'être*, gave a ball that night at the hotel. As all the bedrooms on our floor led on to an open balcony round the ballroom, we had a wonderful glimpse of the dazzling scene. I was struck at once by the great physical beauty of the young Scandinavians. They seemed to glow with the radiance of the warmth and sunlight which they had absorbed during the summer. The particularly brilliant blue worn by the Swedish Air Force was a perfect foil for the low-cut, light-coloured dresses worn by the tanned girls.

Noticing me gazing wistfully at them, some of the young people beckoned to me to join them, but as I was not in full evening dress and had no place at a table, I did not dare to go forward.

My uncle offered to take us out to dinner at a new restaurant in a side-street just off the quay. When we came out of the hotel a strange thing happened. A huge man was standing close to the main front door—so close that I took him to be a hall porter off duty talking to the one who was on. But much to our surprise he followed us as we went down the quay, and coming so close as to almost breathe down our necks, he remarked in a menacing Swedish-American voice, 'So that's how the rich spend their time.'

My uncle, who seemed tiny beside this strange belligerent giant, gave a quick look of disapproval over his shoulder and scuttled on. I was longing to stop and explain that I was not rich at all, only a poor student from the London School of Economics, and that I greatly objected to even being mistaken for a member of the ranks of the rich. But fear that this might lead to an altercation with my uncle led me to desist. As we walked, however, this strange personality moved even closer, apparently unsatisfied by our lack of response. I was beginning to become terribly worried, but providence seemed to come to the rescue when a hefty-looking young Swede stepped from a block of flats into our path. He turned our way and walked along almost beside us. The menacing stranger sheered off. His form no longer overshadowed us and he seemed to fade from our immediate view as we turned thankfully in at the door of the restaurant.

Later, when we had got back safely to the hotel—I don't

recall how, but probably we took a taxi—the atmosphere seemed more tense than ever. There were murmurs about what had come over on the late news, but we could get only a partial account from one of the waiters and a guest who spoke little English.

When we reached our bedroom we found some enormous safety pins laid out by the chambermaid. We were asked to use them to pin the heavy bedroom curtains together and shut in the light. Even neutral Sweden had decided to hold a trial blackout.

We descended the stairs again in a state of acute apprehension, and almost automatically followed the other guests as they swept out in a kind of united impulse through the great swing doors. It was an extraordinary experience suddenly to be precipitated into the street, over which was flung a great mantle of darkness. People were milling around, bumping into one another, and talking in languages I could not understand. I tried frantically to find my mother and uncle, seizing an arm here or there only to find it was not theirs. Finally, by asking for them in English loudly, they heard my voice amidst the general mêlée and we somehow came together again.

Having found each other we stood and gazed at the scene. Our eyes had become accustomed to the dark and sufficiently adjusted to see that over the horizon the moon was rising and turning the water into a glistening silver sheen. The magnificent block of the Royal Palace and other familiar landmarks stood out black and stark against the horizon, munificent on each island with the water winding in between. There was not one garish street lamp to disturb the natural beauty of contour. Never had Stockholm looked so lovely.

Back in the hotel afterwards my uncle took the decision that we must return home, for he felt war was imminent. Although it was after midnight we set to work and packed. In the small hours of the morning, when our task was done and we were ready for bed, we took the great safety pins out of the curtains to try to let in a little fresh air. There was a car park opposite, and standing by the entrance, gazing up at our window, was the tall belligerent stranger who had followed us when we had gone out. Whether he was there at that particular spot by accident or design we never knew, but somehow we had a horrible feeling of being followed, and were suddenly glad to be leaving this city, magnificent though it was.

As originally planned, we took the train across Norway to catch the boat home from Bergen. We had been anxious to make the interesting journey across Sweden and Norway, especially to see the scenic beauty of the Norwegian mountains, but we were in little mood for them now.

We had to spend about two hours in Oslo between trains and made a sortie up the main street as far as one of the famous tourist hotels, where we took a hurried conventional dinner. It was a grey evening, with the chill of winter already in the air. We felt strangers and unattracted by the place. How widely one's impressions of a city can differ. That night Oslo seemed to me a stern, grey place, monotonous and almost ugly, the embodiment of our dark apprehensions and stern forebodings on the international situation. How different it looked when I went there again one glorious day in early summer the year after the liberation when the lilacs were out on the castle hill, and laburnums decked the leafy Studentelunden, and young people lingered leisurely under the trees. Everyone was full of joy at regaining their country and appreciation for the English, anxious to show them around their treasured places, making friendships that have lasted many years. How could I ever have thought it a grim and unfriendly country?

After a night journey through the mountains, obscured by darkness, for it was late in the summer, we set sail from Bergen and reached England at last. Our arrival was met by the English newspapers telling us that the crisis was over. Chamberlain had made an agreement with Hitler and the danger of war seemed to fade into the background.

21

A pattern of prophecy is revealed

Had we looked up the records of our sittings over previous years at this time we should have found a strange chain of statements about future international events which, viewed in sequence, undoubtedly foretold much that was to take place. Having gone through these recently, I set out quotations from them to provide a full picture.

They began in very early years, long before even the possibility of a war had been mooted in the news. Ralph and my father began to speak of disturbances and upheavals, a war condition, and so forth. They evidently linked these with an insight into the post-war period, for they spoke of a whole pattern of new thought and conditions to follow. They did not appear to see it in great detail—or perhaps were not allowed to see it thus—and so did not indicate the terrible conflagration that was to spring up before the era of new thought could be reached. Perhaps if we had known it might have completely sapped our energy and courage to achieve anything constructive, both before and during the actual combat. Certainly the ugly side was not stressed in their first reference, when, on 11 September 1930, they suddenly said:

> Before you come over here to join me and before Ruth comes there will have been such interesting things you will have experienced on earth. Not just the busy things you are doing now helping people, but he has feeling of rather exciting things out of the ordinary things happening all together—Oh he has got that feeling awfully strongly.

On 4 November 1931 Ralph said:

> You will remember when I first spoke to you I told you there would be rather important things happening on the

> earth. Well they have begun and *our work for the earth has begun.* There may be all kinds of things happening before long.

We then asked, 'What sort of things?' and Feda replied, 'Well difficult times, not that they will affect you personally, but that will happen round you.'

This was quite true in every sense, for we had no close relatives in the forces and economically life remained much the same for us, despite the slump.

> There will be industrial and social troubles, he says, which you will have to take in a way a share in, a part in, though they won't have been actually caused by you.

This also was very true, my later training as a social worker leading me to become steeped in the problems of economic depression.

> Ralph says there will be trouble [Feda continued]. There is going to be a very difficult time, a very difficult time and we have got to be prepared. He says there will be a good deal of hardship to many people while things are working themselves out in the right direction. At the same time he and Daddy feel there is more hope now than there was ever before. There is more hope and yet there is more difficulty. There will be trouble, he is quite sure of that, riots and trouble that we have got our work cut out in order to save it getting too bad. But it is moving in the right direction that they want it to on the right side but it is making upheavals and we are expecting trouble, it cannot be helped. They are helping everybody who is moving in the right direction. Ralph's father says 'You see it is really moving in the way God wants it to now, but man has made such an awful muddle so far.'
>
> He says there may be work for you to do in an unexpected way. I do not want to go into details dear, but I have a feeling that you have been left here to do something on different lines to anything you would have expected. I could not have done

it owing to my health, but you and Ruth will do it and I shall help you from this side, with Ralph, and we shall find ourselves connected in work that we could never have thought it possible that we could do together.

'What sort of work?' we asked, to which Feda replied:

Well, I don't know what name I can give it but it will be helping people to get a grip of themselves, and a grip on normal conditions. You may have to tell them things about this other life in order to make them look ahead, beyond the difficulties of today, in order to help them keep their hold on sane and normal things of today of their ordinary lives. You may have to tell them tactfully about our side of life here. That may be one thing, but we shall give you strength and shall impress you with the right things to say to them not only over the life to come but to help them to live the life today, because Daddy says there will be a good deal of what you call abnormality, a good deal of excitement and disturbance in which otherwise sensible people will run past themselves. And that is where you and every person who knows the truth will be needed. Ruth will be, you will be and they will have to work through you.

This forecast came very true in every sense. First, the war was for many a great challenge to their belief, and my mother, having none of the parish work to do now as in former days, had much more time to help people individually with knowledge of our sittings and the nature of the next world.

Also we were destined to find ourselves at the end of the war in a house on an estate where there was a huge prisoner-of-war camp in the form of a college for non-Nazi Germans. Through this we found ourselves, especially my mother, for she was home all day, welcoming prisoners home and telling them about our communications. We also organized a weekly study group on spiritual matters run by a member of the Society of Friends, and this I think helped many who had lost their faith in the orthodox Churches.

My mother treated these young men much as she would have her own son, and many of them remained friends for life.

When I recall my parents' super-patriotism during the First World War and our simple bigotry in believing every single German to be wicked, I realize how true Daddy's prophecy was —'You have been left here to do something on different lines to anything you would have expected.' Continuing the sitting, Feda said:

> Daddy is more serious today over things that are happening than he has ever been. It is a very important period you are going through, he says, a very important chapter IN THE WORLD'S HISTORY [The last four words are in capitals to stress their importance.] Daddy says 'I say it very seriously. There will be bright times that will show things are working out in the right direction, but there will also be dark times and things that will happen which may be alarming, but you must tackle them with faith and hope that they are working out in the right direction.
>
> They keep on saying the right direction [Feda continued]. Only that they will be rather frightening while they are there. This country will pull through, there won't be a rebellion here, but things will be difficult while we are doing it.

On 3 May 1933 Daddy again spoke through Feda on the plan of work mapped out for us, and said:

> We are heading towards very important events. You know [he added very typically] how I dislike exaggeration, but I think this, you are heading towards very important events, very important matters in which a great deal of spiritual and I had better say psychical enlightenment will be needed. You will be needed badly for your knowledge and experience.
>
> Oh there is a great deal to be done, Ralph says, on the earth [Feda remarked on 19 October 1934]. So much to be done so much to be altered. The conditions on earth are appalling and we don't know how men, not God, have allowed it to go on.
>
> Daddy says because THEY HAVE NOT BEEN LOOKING AT IT. [These words in capitals were said in my father's own voice, obviously to stress them.] They are walking by, trying not to see it [he stressed].

Ralph then joined in the conversation and said:

That is why I want Ruth to look at it and say she can see it. The people who work for us, the people who see it and hear and register it all and give it out again, those are the people through whom we can do things. He is helping her with what she has got to do and it will be all right, that's what he feels, all right.

On 19 October 1935 Ralph remarked through Feda:

There are big things happening. This is the most important time. Before his father passed over Ralph was telling you that you would live in important times. This is the beginning of very important times indeed in the world, and they both know that it will affect you individually, what happens to you will come very much out of world conditions directly or indirectly. It does not affect everybody individually, some people it passes by, but people who are linked up with our side it affects more because we are making a link through you to help world vibrations. Therefore we are linking you on to them. We come to you we pick up something from you, a vibration that will go on your plane to help in other more general conditions. We sensitize your conditions as we use them and therefore what happens to you is affected by the conditions we have used you in order to help.

When my father instead of Feda took control of Mrs Leonard during the sitting, he said:

I have been talking to you all the time through Feda, but when I come myself it seems to make it more personal naturally. Well there are going to be some rather difficult conditions on your side. It is not going to develop into a big thing like the 1914 war. No it is not going to be on those lines at all. I think it is leaving things in the air. It is going to be a war condition for sometime. We shall have to alter our opinions and reconstruct things. I do think it is a most difficult situation. I don't think any of us nations will be very proud of ourselves because I do not think we know where we stand really. If we think we know one day we are not quite sure the next. It is a pitiable condition and I am afraid a good deal of trouble and misunderstanding will come out of it. I think we shall learn the final lesson through this difficult situation. We shall learn a lesson but I do not think we shall be very proud of the way. On our side we think it is an extraordinary thing that all these years since the last war we have not been able to prevent another materializing. Sometimes I think it is only on our plane that people really know what they think.

Here my mother asked after a priest friend who had passed over, and father replied:

He is helping in the same things as we are trying to right earth conditions. We are all concentrating on that now. It is the most important work we can do because if we are not very careful there might be a flare-up and the whole world might be in a state of chaos. It needs all our prayers and concentration.

At our sitting on 31 October 1936 Feda relayed a message from Ralph, saying:

He told you about world war conditions some time ago. He told you and Jim told his people. He said about Spain and Italy, so behindhand in civilization that they would be bound to suffer and make suffering for others. There is the decadent country, Spain is, cruel and behind the times. They are bound to suffer and it is not finished yet. Oh, there is a lot more. Ralph says, 'You know, don't you, that we are both helping with it. We got your thoughts about it. You wondered if we were helping. Yes, we are helping. We are doing everything we can about it.'

RUTH: It seems as if things have gone back.

FEDA: Yes, but look, they are only going back in the backward places . . . here . . . they are going ahead in this country.

Never mind, that drop (in ocean) matters. Never mind the drop. Think of it as the axle by which the rest goes, and it is most important that the axle should be kept oiled, and we are oiling it, but Fascism, militarism, are destructive. Isn't it a nuisance. People and their old shirts . . . always talking about shirts, so stupid.

MRS PLANT: They seem to be wrecking other countries.

FEDA: Very stupid people bothering about shirts at all. Well, Ralph says it is a wave, an extreme wave.

RUTH: He thinks it will die down?

FEDA: It will find its level after a great deal of trouble, and don't look for things to be too easy in this country, but this country will keep clearer than most countries. We are going to work in this country. This country is the axle so we have got to work around it, attend to it. It will be better than most places.

It is only on looking back over these communications as a whole that I realize how clearly they pointed not only to international disturbances, but also to definite war. Such thoughts were not in our minds in the least at that time. We were concerned only for peace. We did not believe war would really come until the eleventh hour. Therefore certain dreams and impressions that I received later seem all the more remarkable. But these will be dealt with in due course. Meanwhile, history moved on and we came nearer to the great international catastrophe.

The year after our visit to Stockholm we set out for Norway once more, this time to Balholm on the Sogne Fjord, one of the places we had visited on our first cruise. Balholm was famous for artists, and also for the fact that in the old days the German fleet used to call there in the summer with the Kaiser on board. He used to stay with an artist friend called Dahl, who had a studio by the fjord. He was very nearly left behind there in 1914, for the fleet only sailed on the eve of war.

We stayed up the Esse Fjord, a tributary of the Sogne, at a little guest-house built of wood, called Esse bottom sythe hythe. This complicated name means, I believe, 'Esse mountain hut in the bottom', to translate it literally. It had an exquisite situation just under a mountain which had the picturesque name of the Golden Apple. The guest-house was built on a rocky piece of land on the edge of the fjord. The balcony jutted right out over the water and we could sit in the sun and enjoy our coffee, gazing deep down into the intense green and surrounded by complete peace.

The fjord terminated a little way beyond the hut, and the mountains curved round to make a strange crucible for any sound, which echoed to and fro in the vast enclosure. But there was little to disturb the empty silence other than the panting engine of some small boat, travelling to a farm further up the fjord or taking sightseers for a trip over the water.

It was with amazement, therefore, that we heard one day another engine with a curious insidious purr, differing ominously from the sound of the local boats as the growl of a tiger does from the purr of a domestic cat. Looking up we were astonished to see that a great battleship had glided into the fjord. It loomed up like some vast landslide across the open water. It had all happened so suddenly and almost silently. Had we only known it was truly prophetic of things to come: history was indeed repeating itself.

The ship was the flagship the *Diether von Raeder*. She carried a large crew, and from then on life changed considerably at the quiet little *saeter hytte*. The place was invaded by finely built, sun-tanned young men who sat about on the balcony in their spare time, drinking and singing German songs.

It was mostly ratings and petty officers who came to Essebottom; the senior officers, who looked more severe and difficult to know, went to the grander tourist hotel in Balholm. The sailors who came to Essebottom seemed to welcome rather than shun contacts with other nationals. Now quite changed in our attitude to foreigners, my mother and I made friends among them. As none of us spoke more than a few words of the other's language, communication was difficult, but even so it was surprising how we managed to establish a rapport. One young man especially attached himself to us. He used to come and sit at our table with his friends as soon as he came into the guest-house. His name was Klemens Mass, and he came from the Baltic port of Swenemunde. He invited us to the ship's Open Day, when we were shown round this extraordinary mountain of steel with its endless gadgets all connected with death. As the naval officer son of a friend once remarked, 'The modern battleship is the prostitution of scientific knowledge.'

The cruise was not for them a time of leisure and mere routine. During their stay in port they had stern hours of drilling, manning the guns, and so on, dressed in their pure white uniforms, an odd form of battledress. When we spoke of war they shook their heads. No, there would be no war, they said. I believe that most of us genuinely thought this was true. Up there in peaceful Norway it seemed so unbelievable, so outside current thought, for Norway had fought no one for over a hundred years. The sun shone on the fjord ceaselessly. We had seldom seen such lovely weather there before. The carefree summer days went by until, one evening, Klemens announced he must say good-bye as the ship was sailing next day.

I did not therefore attach any great importance to our farewell in this peaceful land. Here was a nice, pleasant young man who seemed to have enjoyed the company of two women, though they were considerably older than himself. If our friendship had helped a little towards international understanding, we were glad of it, and who knows, we might run up against each other some day in another port in this age of international travel. It was probably '*Auf Wiedersehen*' rather than 'Farewell'.

He stopped to say good-bye to us in the hall, and I can still see how he held out his hand at the bottom of the stairs, shook ours warmly and then turned on his heel. As he went towards the door, I experienced a queer feeling difficult to describe. It was as if time stood still or even did not exist. Suddenly I felt that that moment had been taken out of time. It seemed almost as if the episode was suspended, as if it had always existed and would never disappear. As Klemens strode quickly towards the door and was lost to our sight, I felt that I should always remember this moment because it had some significance far beyond what it seemed to hold in its present setting.

I little knew that, in a short space, Norway's hundred years of peace would be broken, that she would be occupied by Germany and that, after a fierce battle with the British Navy, *Diether von Raeder* would lie at the bottom of Narvik Fjord. Some of the crew managed to swim to shore when she sank. Whether Klemens was among those saved I never knew.

We left Balholm a few days later, and when we reached Bergen *en route* for home learnt that Hitler had occupied Danzig.

13

The clouds gather and the storm breaks

Safely back in England we still did not accept the possibility of war. We felt that while there might be very protracted negotiations and anxious situations, war on an extensive scale seemed unthinkable.

On our return we went to stay with some old friends near our former home in the Midlands. They lived in a delightful old house on a steep wooded hillside which the house was literally built into. Our bedroom, though on the first floor, was next door to the room our doctor host had made his surgery, and it was on the same level as the stable yard, so steep was the gradient. I realize now that psychic conditions were probably particularly strong in those surroundings, not only because of the age of the house, but because of its close contact with the magnetic power of the earth.

Our room was old-fashioned and delightful, decorated in shades of mellow lilac. It was dominated by a huge canopy bed, a family heirloom. Every evening the manservant used to light a fire in the old black iron grate, to make the room warm for us when we went to wash before dinner. By bedtime the fire was dying down a little and one might lie cosily watching the flickering flames and the dancing shadows on the wall.

Lying one night in this state of relaxed contemplation we were rudely aroused by a sudden thud. To our amazement the sash window dropped open as far as it could go, the door swung open for no reason at all and the whole front of the grate, including the mantelpiece, fell forward and crashed on to the floor.

We leapt out of bed to try to rectify matters, fearing that the whole grate itself might follow suit, and with it the live coals. Then, suddenly, the ridiculousness of the situation dawned on us. We laughed so much we could hardly lift the heavy fireplace again, but we did achieve this with a great effort and propped it against the wall at a steep angle, hoping it might help to hold back the grate itself.

The cause of this sudden cataclysm remained a mystery. We thought at first that perhaps a gust of wind had shaken the house, but we had felt no gust ourselves when we came to consider the idea. Considering it now, with more understanding, I think that it may well have resulted from a build-up of psychic conditions in that old room, for the power that had accumulated was later manifested in some precognitive dreams which I had there.

I call these dream experiences for want of a better term, though actually they took place on that strange borderland between sleeping and waking where one often becomes supersensitive to the unseen. In each case, as far as I can recall, I had woken up early, about 5 or 6 a.m., probably because of anxiety about the international situation. But the peace of the old room and the cosy comfort of the curtained bed probably had a soporific effect and caused me to drop back in a doze. It was then that the dreams commenced.

The first was about our friend in the German Navy, and it is important to know that shortly before I had written him a letter recalling our happy time in peaceful Norway and saying how sorry I was that the situation had grown so tense, and how much I hoped it would not come to war. From what we heard on the news bulletins about German mobilization and general conditions there, it seemed unlikely that the letter would get through to him. Klemens was therefore much in my thoughts, and it did not seem surprising when I saw him suddenly coming towards me in my dream and we each stretched out a hand in greeting. But just before our hands met a bugle sounded loudly somewhere near by. He stopped abruptly, clicked his feet together and listened.

'I'm sorry,' he said, 'my country needs me, I must go.'

As he turned on his heel and strode away, I suddenly recalled his departure at Balholm and realized the similarity. Then I knew why that episode had held such a deep significance and had seemed to stand forth out of time. As I gazed after him I realized that he was dressed in white uniform, which to me symbolized battledress, and as I looked about me I discovered that we were surrounded by dense jungle, which frightened me. It symbolized the primitive chaos of war, I presume, but I did not realize it then.

Subsequently the international news grew worse and worse, but both my mother and I remained convinced that no actual war would come. Then, another morning, at about the same time and in the same place, I heard my brother's voice speaking to me and saying, 'Things are going to get so bad from now onwards that you will think there is never going to be peace again, so I want to show you something to reassure you.'

I found myself sitting in a train, which I felt was travelling to the Newcastle on Tyne Commission, where we took the boat from to Norway. I often did this train journey in normal life, and even then the boat train would go very fast and rock alarmingly. Near the quay it would be delayed by odd shuntings to and fro, which always proved frustrating when one was eager to board the boat and get under way.

In my dream the train showed all these characteristics, but they were more intense and exaggerated. Not only did it go terribly fast, but it travelled up and down steep inclines with the recklessness of a scenic railway. I was filled with the same terror and amazement as I would have when travelling on one, laughing with relief on finding after each ghastly plunge that we remained on the line.

Not only did the train go backwards and forwards, but it appeared to emulate the actions of a snake, twisting back and forth all over the countryside. Somehow I could see its course on the map detachedly at the same time as sitting in it.

Between its bursts of activity the train came to a complete halt, and we were forced to sit in great apprehension, saying to each other, 'What on earth is going to happen next?'

Then, finally, the train seemed to work up to a crescendo, becoming even faster and more erratic than before. It made one last desperate dash and came to an abrupt standstill simply because it had reached the coastline and could go no further. I looked out and saw Newcastle on Tyne written in large letters across the sea. My brother's voice said reassuringly and emphatically, 'You *will* get to Newcastle in the end.' Now,

Newcastle symbolized for me the gateway to Norway and the entry into the kingdom of peace and happiness.

Still, I queried that one could come through such a dreadful episode intact. I turned and asked my brother how this might really be possible. Then I heard him speaking in his quiet reassuring way the characteristic phrase, 'All will be well I tell you, and again all will be well.' As I have said, I did not then know that this phrase, which he so often used when either mother or I became alarmed, was based on the saying of the famous mystic Julian of Norwich.

During the ensuing years I was able to hold on to the memory of my vivid dream in the darkest moment of war, when international and personal anxiety came almost beyond bearing. I thought of it when reassuring my despairing Norwegian friends when France fell and it looked as though they might never return to their beloved land. It gave me an immense sense of security when international events seemed to take a plunge into the abyss, even as the switchback railway had done. 'All will be well and you will get to Newcastle in the end,' I said to myself over and over. And I was not disillusioned. It all came perfectly true at the right time, but of this I will say more later.

Seeing the pattern of the war as a whole one can see the similarities in my dream: the lightning campaigns which Hitler carried out all over the map, invading one country after another, the fierce, rapid fighting to occupy each country and then the ominous lull between each attack while he gathered the strength to strike again. Had I envisaged a war in the immediate future—and at the time I had the dream I still imagined that when Ralph spoke of these hectic conditions he meant a prolonged period of critical international negotiations—I should have thought of a war pursuing the patterns of that of 1914–18, a bitter struggle over a comparatively small area of land endlessly changing hands with the stubborn fighting of the armies of the major powers.

It seems therefore that there was evidence here of an entity outside my mind, endowed with precognition, who was the author of this extraordinary revelation which had seemed during the preceding period so unlikely to be fulfilled.

We returned to London a few days after I had this dream,

disturbed and disappointed by the news. I suppose I was still questioning the future regarding the international situation, and it was as a result of this that I experienced another dream. In this one I was caught into the air and floating high above the earth, but able to view it much as if I had been in a plane. I recall seeing a town with a church tower and other projecting landmarks, and suddenly I realized that the whole earth seemed welded together in a density as solid as if it was a huge cliff instead of an area of human habitation. Homes and Church seemed to be bogged down in it, and the people in them. I felt that the person who accompanied me on this journey was making a kind of test, and when they tested the atmosphere and saw how solidly opaque and insensitive it was, they shook their heads and indicated that nothing could be done. The inevitable must follow because of man's insensitivity to the situation, I suppose they meant, but it was rather like a doctor saying with professional tact that the verdict on a patient was 'incurable'. Concrete facts regarding the future were avoided. So, in my heart, I still hoped that some miraculous change would take place before an irretrievable declaration of war.

It was perhaps appropriate that, on the fatal Sunday morning of 3 September 1939, we should have been at morning service in St Martin-in-the-Fields. We had lived close by the church for many years in a flat just by its east end, and the vicar, the Rev. Pat McCormick, and his family were well known to us. We had a sense of belonging there in times of crisis. Before the service the vicar came out of the vestry and announced that the news was very bad, but that there was still a slight hope of negotiations through a last-minute note from Chamberlain to Hitler. We should know finally in about half an hour, and he would come and tell us the result.

The service proceeded as usual, with one of the curates officiating, though had we been able to see into the minds of the congregation all would have seemed very distrait, I think. About half an hour later the vestry door opened and the vicar entered. He stepped into the pew used by the clergy and came to the end of it nearest the congregation. Then he turned to face us. He was an imposing figure, broad and tall, his head bald on top but with a frill of reddish curly hair turning white round the edge. His normally pink complexion was a little more intense than usual. The bright red of his cassock (St Martin's was a royal church) seemed enhanced by the ivory whiteness of his surplice as he turned to speak. The congregation waited in tense silence, every eye focused on him, as the sound of the organ died away. Then he spoke slowly and clearly the fatal words, 'No reply has come to Mr Chamberlain from Adolf Hitler so I regret to say *we are at war with* Germany.'

After this there was silence while everyone stood still dazedly, wondering what the future held. We did not know then that our clergyman friend would die from a heart attack one night after a very bad blitz, this and many nights of ministering to the hundreds of people who crowded into his crypt having put too much strain on his failing strength.

Our first sitting after the outbreak of war was on my mother's birthday, 19 October. It immediately started with Ralph and father sending emphatic messages denouncing the war as entirely against God's plans and due to the wilfulness of men. This appeared further to emphasize my dream about the terrible opaqueness surrounding mankind on the earth.

> They are very busy [Feda said] trying to do all they can to help these wretched conditions, as much as they can. They want you to go on helping with thoughts and prayers for peace because this war is against our plans, entirely against our plans. As we told you before there are certain plans for things ordained by God and it is entirely man's wilfulness that has allowed or caused this to happen.

Then Feda added her characteristic, and rather playful-sounding phrase, 'Int it noosence?' To which Ralph replied, with his rather characteristic earnestness and dignity, 'It isn't a nuisance it's a tragedy. We want you to help,' he continued, 'because if you can't help it going on you can help to stop it at the right time and get a better peace.'

I replied to this, 'It is difficult to pray now there seems no point to focus on. Should one pray for peace now and end this terrible thing, or pray that it may go on till everyone has seen the utter futility of it?'

Feda replied:

> Let God work it out. All you have to do is to link up with God for the purpose of peace. We often make a mistake in prayer by dictating the details, let it be His own way in His own time. Prayer will make Peace come quicker and in the right way.

Regarding our own personal life at this time, he had something to say, quite unasked for. Feda was talking about an old family house in Cheshire when suddenly she broke off and asked:

> What did you say Ralph? Well he hardly knows how to put it because things are rather betwixt and between for you both just now. Things and friendships are going out which may affect both you and Ruth. It seems that you are in touch with people that may (he won't say must in these problematical conditions) may lead to things, he keeps on saying for you as well as Ruth. You won't just stand by and say this is good for Ruth. There are many people on earth you can help, not only Ruth.
>
> Is Ruth thinking of some work with a band of people?

'Yes,' I replied, 'I have just applied to the Quakers for some work.'

'Well,' Feda went on, 'I feel she is going to get it.'

I said, 'Well I have just refused an offer from them to work in a community out of town and I wondered if I should have accepted and gone away.'

'No,' Feda replied. 'They feel you need not go away in fact it might not be right. They did not want you to accept what is offered now. Something more important may come along later if you are on the spot.'

This proved very true. Though this work did not materialize till over two years later, it proved one of the most exciting jobs I have had and was the key to a whole new field of work opening out from it. I mention this because it shows how important it is to wait with patience and discipline till the right opening can come at the right time.

In its early days the war was described as a 'phoney war'.

Little happened to disturb the peace of our island. It seemed immune behind its physical barrier of sea. My mother and I went to live in the house of Dr David Briggs, a friend in London, his wife Joy having been evacuated with their baby daughter for fear of bombs that had never come. She was a close friend of ours, being niece of Mr Drayton Thomas, who had got us the first messages from Ralph, and daughter of Etta, with whom he first communicated. As they lived at Highgate we were able to get into town easily and I took up work teaching refugees English and running lunch clubs and discussion groups for them.

By the following summer, however, this work came to an end, while Joy, impatient with her apparently unnecessary exile, no bombs having dropped, wanted to return to her home. We therefore had to decide on a move to a new place. We went for a sitting with Mrs Leonard on 19 July at her home, The Haven, where she now lived on the Kent coast. During it my father, taking control, spoke of the war and said, 'We are with you, helping you, you have got to keep your mind on the future and get through it all. We know all the difficulties. We want to do our best all round. Just go on quietly.'

My mother then asked, 'Will there be great loss of life before it is over?'

My father replied, 'There is bound to be loss of life and difficulties, as in the first war, but it won't be so long.'

This latter remark proved inaccurate as the war was to last for some years. It is interesting that the one thing on which those on the Other Side seem to go wrong often is when they try to forecast the duration of events. Since they live outside the time sphere they are probably unable to sense its vibrations accurately.

My father continued:

> But I want to say that there will be some change in the policy of the government this autumn. What we are trying to do is to impress people to put up some home defences. If we can tire them out it will be all right, and we shall tire them out.

On looking through a history book I see that the Battle of Britain had virtually started two days before this, on 10 July, when a number of mass bombing raids were made on airfields in the south. But ordinary civilians like us had not the slightest idea that these raids had any special significance. Nor could we foresee that the defence put up by our fighter squadrons in the Battle of Britain and over London during the winter blitz was to be such a vital factor. Not only did the blitz begin to peter out by the spring, but Hitler changed his mind about many things to do with this island, including his attitude to the possibilities of a successful invasion. It was this that probably tipped the scales in our favour when such an action became apparently militarily favourable through the collapse of France. Undoubtedly they on the Other Side saw much further and more clearly into the future than we then did.

My mother asked the question, 'Is it not right to make peace yet?' My father replied:

> We want peace, but it won't be made at present no matter what we think. We shall tire out the people we have for the moment to call our enemies, and we shall *all* have learnt some very bitter lessons at the end of it. It is awful my dear [he said turning to my mother] that you should have to go through another war. And it is people's fault the older ones have allowed things to slide. We have not made the right conditions that would have made war impossible.
>
> In spite of all that is happening however [he went on] we have never been so busy nor so confident in the future, and we wanted to see you to tell you that. When the cloud has passed we shall establish with you a new world order. It won't be like the last war forgetting a year after. You see this is quite a different sort of war; other wars have been fought on foreign soil, Africa or even France. We were only fighting a few weeks in France this time, and now it has come to England. But there will be a great spiritual growth and better conditions ultimately for everyone, not just for some. If you can get through the present, and we are helping all we can, we shall be all right.

Looking back over the years it looks as though much of this is being fulfilled. Thought and even social structure has changed enormously, but the birth-pangs of this new world order are still troubling the world years later, which only seems to emphasize my father's remark, 'This won't be like the last world war forgetting a year after.'

14

New surroundings

During our sitting in July my mother asked a personal question about our own lives as she was concerned about where we should live when we left Highgate.

My father replied, 'Don't worry, leave everything at present. It is a matter of just carrying on from week to week.'

Being of a rather anxious planning nature, however, my mother unfortunately did not accept this. So she did exactly the opposite. She went to the unnecessary trouble of looking for rooms in London and booking them for the autumn. As the war situation and our own plans developed we realized that her action was not fitting into the overall pattern. We had to cancel the rooms ultimately and pay some compensation, which all goes to prove what a mistake it is to fail to recognize the importance of such things and to utilize the information if it is given to us.

As it was still summer we decided to spend a few weeks at the Quakers' Hostel at Jordans. It lay within easy reach of London for some reporting work I had taken on for the Quakers and provided a peaceful and interesting environment for my mother while I was away in the daytime.

Our connection with Jordans, which was to prove so helpful and permanent, like so many of our important links came about through a chance remark and a series of quite unexpected circumstances. Living in London during the winter we had joined a working party at the vicarage of St Martin's in the Fields. While sitting quietly sewing one day I overheard a colonel's wife a few places away telling the vicar's wife of a particularly pleasant week-end she and her husband had spent at a place called Old Jordans Hostel. Some weeks later this information suddenly came into use when we had to cancel a week-end with friends in Oxfordshire because their married son and his family wanted to come and stay. Determined that my overworked mother should not miss her week-end in the country, I succeeded in arranging rooms at Jordans at short notice.

Our chance week-end visit, which we greatly enjoyed, proved like our visit to Norway to be an essential link in the chain. During our brief stay at the hostel we had made friends with some refugees from Frankfurt-am-Main, Mr and Mrs Friedlander. When we returned to Jordans for our summer holiday they had moved into a cottage in the village and had come to know many people there, which was to stand us in good stead.

Safely ensconced in the hostel for two weeks, time passed very peaceably during those lovely late days. The sunk garden proved a wonderful place for typing out my reports. It provided shelter from the cold autumn winds, and even the chill winds of war seemed to have receded into the background until, one Saturday night, the storm burst. We had been to see friends on the outer edge of the village, and as we came out of their house late after dark saw the horrific glow from thousands of fires thirty miles away. The City of London was once again on fire. But it was no domestic affair due to vulnerable wooden buildings, such as that Pepys had seen, but an invasion by a powerful air force from another country and an episode that was to recur many times in the months ahead.

Our time at the hostel was nearly up and we had intended to return to London, but now our good friends, the Friedlanders, intervened. Why should we go back to the dangers of London when we could just as easily take a room in the village and go up to London for the day to undertake any work we had to carry out? Mrs Friedlander called for us one morning and took us firmly round the village knocking on the doors of all those people they knew and asking if they or anyone else could take us in as paying guests. After several failures we came to a house which had a particular appeal. Its sloping roof and wooden ends were in imitation of a house in Norway. The family were sitting out on the lawn of luscious grass under an apple tree laden with bright red crab apples. It was rather reminiscent of those gatherings we had seen beside the fjord when passing by boat. The owners invited us to stay to elevenses. We talked for some time, finding matters of mutual interest, and when we were invited to stay on and slice the beans for lunch we felt we had been accepted into the family. In this we were right, for we were offered rooms for six weeks until some other friends, who had booked previously, were due to arrive.

The occupants were two Scotch sisters—one the widow of a Dutchman and the other married to a Czech, who was the third occupant of the house, a delightful elfin little man with whom we were to become great friends. The house was beautifully built and furnished and ornamented with gaily painted Czech objects. Interesting people came and went from many nations, including the charming sister of President Beneš and her Swiss doctor husband.

Having found such a wonderful haven for ourselves, we began to worry over Mrs Leonard's Haven which was not now so well placed. The war had taken the active turn prophesied and Tankerton, the town where she lived on the Kent coast, was heavily involved in the new defences forecast by those on the Other Side. At the tip of the Thames Estuary, it was where the fighters came out to meet the bombers invading from the sea. Many of the worst aerial combats were fought over it. My mother, with her usual great concern for people, became aware of the urgent need to move her to a safer place and took on the task of trying to find a furnished house near to us.

This was likely to prove difficult, for now that the blitz had started in earnest everyone was flying out to this commuter country to the north-west, so handy for London and on the quietest side. Nevertheless, since Gladys's need was so particularly urgent owing to the nature of her work, we hoped and prayed that if we really made the effort some door might open for her miraculously. We were not disappointed.

When we heard that the Battle of Britain was intensifying we set out in a great hurry to the neighbouring town of Amersham to search for a house. We did not stay to dress in our best clothes or even to put on hats. We had heard of a well-known house agent in that town who might be able to help. When we reached the office we were amazed to see that there was actually one house advertised 'To let' in the window, a rare thing in those days. We marched jubilantly in, thinking that this might be our miracle.

But the conventional secretary behind a typewriter shook her head. 'I already have thirty names down for that particular house,' she explained. 'There would be no point in adding more.' Had we accepted her very practical but negative attitude and gone away without further discussion a whole train of events might have been frustrated. Remembering the insistence of those on the Other Side about their power to help if we knocked on all doors, I persisted in asking that our name should at least be put on the list, despite the apparent lack of hope.

Finally the girl acquiesced rather, I suppose, than offend a client, and she put our names down. As we turned to go the head of the firm happened to open his office door and come out. We said good morning and he opened the street door for us and bowed us out. We hardly exchanged two words.

When we got back to our rooms in Jordans the phone rang. It was the estate agent, offering us the house. Would we come over and see it? Of course we would. We went back straight away.

'What made you pick on us?' we asked when we had viewed it and taken on it Mrs Leonard's behalf. 'We were just bemoaning the fact that we had not dressed up more smartly to come to see you.'

'But that is exactly why I chose you,' he replied. 'Smart people give parties and burn my clients' covers and spill drink on them. You looked exactly the type I was looking for.'

We just could not believe our luck. No one else could. The rather dominating lady in whose house we had taken rooms after the six weeks allotted us at the Czechs' house were over simply could not understand it. She expressed the opinion that there must be a snag in it of some sort; there was probably a dead body locked up in the small bedroom which the owners had kept shut, apparently to store their things in. Such a suggestion was hardly tenable about the respectable retired Harley Street specialist and his wife who usually lived there. We felt that we had a perfectly satisfactory explanation in that we had been granted an answer to our prayers and urgent wish to get Gladys Leonard away from the great danger of living in a battle area.

That our action was well-timed and done unconsciously at

the behest of, and in co-operation with, those who took care of her is shown by a quotation from Gladys Leonard's book *Brief Darkness*, which she wrote shortly after:

> Travelling backwards and forwards from my home on the Kentish coast to London soon became very difficult. The Battle of Britain was in full swing, but I made up my mind to see it through and stay in my home as long as possible. This I managed to do, in spite of the fact that it entailed living in a state of constant unrest and excitement until the end of October, when I received some urgent messages from the Other Side through two different quarters. One came from Mrs Plant, a friend with whom I had been sitting for several years, though usually at rather long intervals. She wrote me and implored me to leave the dangerous neighbourhood in which I lived and to go for a time to a furnished house in a quieter locality which she had seen, and which could be had at a very reasonable rent. By the same post came a letter from Miss Helen MacGregor, whose sterling psychic powers are known to many people. She strongly urged me to leave as soon as possible, and said that the Guides had already arranged something for me, and that I must take it, for I should suffer physically and psychically if I persisted in staying in my home under present conditions. She said that I did not realize the harm that was being done to my nervous system. This was quite true, as I rather prided myself on being able to keep calm and cheerful, no matter what happened. This message from Miss MacGregor was evidential as well as helpful. She could not have known that Mrs Plant had just found a house for me, and she had never met Mrs Plant herself.

Just before Gladys arrived at the new house she was told psychically that she might not find conditions quite good there, but that it would lead to something good. This proved correct. The first night she was there a bomb dropped in a garden horribly close, which made her feel that it was not such a quiet haven after all.

She brought with her to share the house a number of relatives who lived close to her in Kent. After a time they grew restless and preferred to go back to their old home. We had meanwhile been asked to leave our rooms, so Gladys invited us to share her house, and from then on began a close friendship which has never been broken over all these years.

Those were, in spite of the strain of war, idyllic days in that small, rather stuffy little house of stockbrokers' Tudor, enclosed discreetly by high hedges. It was winter, and every evening we drew the curtains and ate a cosy supper together—often some delicious vegetarian meal new to us and cooked by Gladys. Like many people who have been on the stage she liked her meal late. We therefore used to get into our dressing gowns first and then sit comfortably round the fire. For entertainment we listened with great amusement to that famous political commentator 'Lord Haw-Haw' broadcasting from Germany. We gained no dangerous despondency but much entertainment from this occupation. I still recall some of his phrases such as, 'I hear the shipping lists from England to America are full. The Pluto rats are leaving the sinking ship.'

We also talked much with Gladys in those long evenings about psychic matters and what our friends on the Other Side thought on so many things. There was always something of the joy and excitement of the explorer about her as she related to us the signposts that had been revealed to her on the way and the routes they seemed to point to as she interpreted them. So entertained were we by these convictions that we took little notice of things in this world, especially not an enemy bomber that seemed oddly to circle overhead each night. It had only once dropped anything, so it did not worry us. We little knew that a strange ugly-looking pile a mile out of town was in reality an ammunition dump, which was probably why the owner of the house and his wife had fled north.

Many sitters came and went at the house by day. I do not think that anyone, not even the agent, ever knew exactly what Gladys's work was. (He had been reassured of her respectability by references from two well-known titled ladies.) Perhaps some of the suburban neighbours got rather a surprise one day when Sir Oliver Lodge's son came to see her. Gladys looked out of the window and, seeing him moving towards the tradesmen's entrance, called out, 'The other gate, Brodie.' With quick humour he called back in a very audible voice, 'Oh I see, Gladys, the ghosts go to the left.'

When we finally left the house, the owners having decided to come back in March and risk the bombs, our agent friend must have been further mystified when having to forward to Gladys a farewell telegram from Mackenzie King sent as the Canadian prime minister left for home. In it he thanked her for all her work and help during the past months and wished her every success in the future. Gladys chuckled when it arrived at our new address. 'I expect the house agent thinks I am a Secret Service Agent,' she said.

The next move was, as always, signposted for us. Gladys had been asked to go to the Lake District to give a series of sittings at Rydal Mount, which had once been Wordsworth's home. She invited us to accompany her. We travelled to Grasmere and stayed in a vegetarian guest-house for a few weeks while looking for somewhere to live, for it seemed almost impossible to get anything near London at present. Gladys was invited to look at some rooms in the house of one of her sitters.

On the way to their house we paused at the studio of the lakeland artist, Heaton Cooper. Viewing his pictures I remarked to my mother about one, 'How wonderfully like Norway that is, yet it must be the Lake District really as Mr Heaton Cooper painted it.' At that very moment the artist must have entered the studio, and overhearing the remark he came over to us and said, 'That is not my picture it is my father's. You are quite right, it is Norway. It is a place called Balholm, where my father and mother met, fell in love and were married there at the English Church. She is Norwegian.'

'Balholm,' we said. 'We know the place well.' We were amazed at this. Here was the famous Balholm coming into our lives again to provide a link.

We thanked him for letting us see his pictures and then passed on to our friend's house up the road. On the way up the drive Gladys suddenly saw a young girl in the spirit standing beside her. She was puzzled by this. She asked the people she was visiting if they could identify her, but they said no, they had no clue as to her identity. The rooms proved unsuitable for her use, so the visit was brief.

When we returned to the village I remarked that the usual way to find accommodation was to buy a local paper. We did so, and much to our surprise at once came across an advertisement for a bungalow. It was to let at a place called Loweswater. We could not believe our luck! But when we came to think things over we realized that, if a house had to be advertised when there was a blitz on London and Liverpool, there might well be something wrong with it to prevent people on the spot taking it. We therefore decided to consult our artist friend again, as his local knowledge might be of use. On showing him the paper he seemed amazed.

'What a strange thing,' he said. 'You came here a short time ago and told me you knew Balholm where my mother and father were married. Now you come and tell me about the place where I spent my own honeymoon. Loweswater is a lovely place. I know the people who own this bungalow. We called them the Happy Ladies. Take a taxi at once and go over and get it before anyone else does.'

We did as instructed, and I shall never forget the sight of that strange little building as we bumped up the rutted lane to the Happy Ladies' cottage. It was hardly a bungalow in the sophisticated sense, but really two army huts from the First World War pushed together with an old-fashioned stove-pipe sticking out of the roof of one of them at a rakish angle. But it lay in the most heavenly surroundings, which made it excel a palace so far as we were concerned.

It was built on the lower slopes of the mountain of Melbrake, which forms part of the mountain range round Crummock Water. Warm bracken covered the lower slopes, backed by oak wood, made up of very old trees that were twisted by the winds of time into strange shapes like trees in a children's fairy-story book. After that the mountain rose sheer, topped by great rocky seams from which swooped the peregrine falcon.

On the other side fields stretched down to the brilliant blue waters of Crummock, which seemed to dance in the sunlight as we looked at them. Every now and then the air was pierced by the full-throated whistles of curlews as they circled overhead and spiralled down into their hiding places in marshes.

The Happy Ladies were just as charming as our artist friend

had said. It appeared that they were Quakers and were delighted to let the bungalow to tenants who came from a place so connected with the Society of Friends as Jordans. The bungalow was free till June. We took it at once.

My mother was the only one who was a little apprehensive about taking The Hut, as we found our domicile was appropriately called, but we allayed her fears and on a bleak March day arrived there in a taxi we had somehow managed to hire (in those days of petrol rationing it was not easy to get one to go on a long journey). It was bitterly cold, and to make things worse we developed colds ourselves. We all retired to bed in our warmest dressing gowns and even wore woollen helmets on our heads to keep out the innumerable small draughts that seemed to permeate the structure at many points. The first morning we awoke to see a skittering of snow over everything. The sparkling beauty of it soon made us forget our bodily discomforts. After all, it was well on in March and was not spring just round the corner?

As time went on and the weather grew warmer we began to see more of the wonderful nature surrounding us and the innumerable birds and animals. Most prolific and insistent were the Cumberland sheep, whose plaintive 'Baas' spread like a vast chorus right across the hills. So often did we hear the sound that we failed to realize a cry for help one day, until we went out and found a lamb lying semi-conscious almost across our doorstep. We did not know then that a sheep is not inevitably endowed with the urgent maternal love and instinct to protect her young expressed in a cat or dog. A young ewe will often walk off and refuse to suckle the lamb to which it has given birth.

We felt the lamb's heart. It was still beating faintly. Instinctively I rushed it to the oven, which only emitted a gentle warmth owing to the inadequate functioning of the ancient stove. I laid it on the shelf, leaving the door wide open for air. It seemed to act as an incubator would for a premature child. Gradually the heart became stronger, the eyes brighter, until the little beast stirred and came wholly back to life.

Taken out of the oven and given a cosy bed by the stove, it soon gained strength and skipped around the room, its funny little black hooves tapping on the old wooden floor like the high heels of a girl's shoes. We found the owner of the sheep and the farmer's son came and fetched it. He said they would bring it up on a bottle on the farm.

It would grow up a domestic pet of the family, no doubt, sheltered and trusting, but when it got to be of material value the principle of loyalty and friendship would soon be forgotten. It would go straight to the slaughter-house for mutton.

It was, in fact, the last lamb we were ever to put in the oven, for soon after we signed a solemn declaration from the Ministry of Health promising to 'abstain absolutely from eating either fish flesh or fowl'. This entitled us to a specially large cheese ration in our book to replace meat. I had at last achieved another of my deep-rooted wishes by becoming a vegetarian. Now I felt that my affection for animals was consistent and free from guilt.

The beauty of spring in the unique surroundings of the Hut was unforgettable. The larch wood by Crummock Water became an intense green, and the trees came to be known among us as 'The Little Larches', almost as if they were a local family. Planted on raised land above the water, their reflections in it were like the towers of fairy castles, a maze of bright green spikes emerging in the smooth waters of the lake.

The best thing about The Hut was the wonderful conditions for sittings. Feda explained that it was the pure atmosphere which created them. I suppose one important point was that it was uncluttered by too many vibrations of thought. The situation is rather similar to when I listen to my small transistor radio late at night. I can, for instance, get opera direct from Milan, a thing I could never do when all the other European stations are on. One of the types of phenomena which benefited most from these conditions was the direct voice. It was amazing to hear Ralph's familiar tone so clear and 'alive' in every sense of the word. I specially recall one occasion when we heard him say to my mother, 'Hullo, darling,' so clearly and naturally beside us that it seemed as if we must see him.

> He is just there [Feda said] walking up and down close to you if only you could see him. He came right up to his mother then.

The quality of the communications was also good in The Hut. On 25 April we received a particularly interesting message about the war.

> This summer [Feda said] for the next three months we shall not know what will happen in one place or another. It is pandemonium made by man, not God's plans, but God's plans will eventually assert themselves. But for the moment evil is top dog. That is what is holding us up.
>
> We don't know what place may suffer, we don't know what place may not. Even beautiful churches are being bombed, we could not prevent it, evil is too predominant.
>
> We feel, however, that at a time which you on earth call midsummer, something will be ready for a climax or have reached it. Some step will be taken which will show as you look back that it had a very great bearing on later events, and even on the end of the war. I don't mean it will be the end of the war but it will have very great bearing on it. You will know much better when the end of the war will be after this.

It is a pity that in those days we had no tape recorder and that I have for evidence only my notes taken in longhand. As I am not a trained shorthand typist they are therefore incomplete, for Feda talked so quickly that it was not possible to keep pace with her and get things down verbatim. But my mother always declared, and she may have been right, that what my brother actually said was, 'A step will be taken by Hitler.' If he did say this it was, of course, a remarkable detailed prophecy. For the sake of complete honesty, however, this addition must remain merely a supposition.

I remember our amazement when, at 1 o'clock on the day after midsummer, we were in the hall at High Cross (where we had taken rooms). The kitchen door flew open and out rushed the owner, Mrs Fearon, carrying a portable wireless set and crying, 'Hitler's invaded Russia, Hitler's invaded Russia!' Her excitement about this decisive move could hardly equal our amazement at the fulfilment of the prophecy. German troops had crossed the Russian frontier one hour after midnight on midsummer night.

Feda had also said during this sitting:

> There is a chance of the war petering out this year, or well before the end of this year. The next two and a half to three months depend on this. If it does not it will go on well into the next year I am afraid. That is our feeling and we think we are right about it.

Studying the history of the war in retrospect, this may now be understood. Hitler imagined he could take Russia before the winter came on, but failed to do so. He had apparently made little provision for the huge army he had placed there to receive winter supplies, warm clothes and other necessities. The army came near to breaking point that first winter, and the war would certainly have petered out had they given in on such an important front.

My father, speaking in direct voice at one of our sittings, said another thing of interest to my mother:

> There is something which may happen which looks like the end of the war, but don't be in a hurry and conclude it has ended because it may break out again, my own dearest. We want to protect you because there are things for you to do. Keep this to yourselves, don't write about it or talk about it to others. I think things are often best kept quiet until they have worked themselves out to a logical conclusion.

This latter was probably an allusion to the rockets that were later to develop, the new secret weapon which Germany would suddenly produce after the normal blitz had died down and we thought we had nothing further to fear from the air.

The sitting we held after Germany's invasion of Russia opened, rather unusually, with an immediate reference to the war.

> They are so glad [Feda said] that you had the sitting as it is a good time to have it, or as good as any. If you had waited a few weeks they still would have not said anything different. We still don't know what turns it will take in the situation

> but whatever turns it will take it will work out to the same result. Don't forget the details of what will happen don't matter.
>
> If the Germans or the Russians have a reverse it won't matter. It will be the balance of things that in the end will matter. Ralph says don't judge anything by present events or happenings.

This was very comforting to know at that particular time, when Hitler held so much of Europe and North Africa and the picture appeared grim.

> I am afraid that Germany will make some headway [Ralph went on], but it will cost them something. They won't get the whole of Russia under their thumbs and what they do get they will be sorry they have got at all. The next five weeks will be very important indeed not only for Russia, but for us. You will understand this later.

This, of course, proved very true, for just like Napoleon's army the German one became exhausted and handicapped by the vast areas they had taken over and for which they had to obtain supplies.

The importance of the next five weeks for England became clear when, perusing the records, I learnt that it was just at this time that the Long Range Desert Group was formed. This was the British foundation stone for the later victorious Eighth Army.

> You want to know how I am [Ralph continued]. I am well and busy, busy not with our own people the English, but with strangers with those of other countries who are just being mown down. We are working in Russia. The havoc is awful. We are helping people on both sides. Many Germans when they come over don't know what they are fighting about, don't realize what they are contributing to, so we are helping them. I have a busy time for as Gladys knows minds have to be healed when bodies have been hurt on Your Side. Tell Gladys she was writing about this and got it right. The effects are pretty bad for a time.

It is a very strange thing but I have been almost waiting since the beginning of the war for this Russian affair to mature, because certain changes will come to England through this. The fact that Russia has entered the war does not only mean that she has come into it as a belligerent, it means she will have a good influence, it may be troublesome, but a good one in the future.

We shall have trouble apart from war, but it will work out all right. Don't talk about it, it is for your own private ears alone. Apart from war there will be troubles and squabbles here about the lines on which to build the country up after the war is over.

This, of course, has proved only too true. We are still in these days working it out.

15

Strange links with the past

That time had come all too shortly for us to move out of our strange little wooden dwelling by the lake so as to make room for the regular holiday let. We were very sorry to leave, for in spite of the primitive accommodation we had been very happy there in that idyllic setting of abundant natural beauty and peace.

We went round the village making our need for new accommodation known. The reception was rather disheartening. Most houses were occupied by farming families with no obligation to take evacuees and too busy to take lodgers. There was one house that particularly attracted us. It was approached by a long avenue of very tall trees running slightly uphill and leading to two stone pillars and a fine wrought-iron gate someone had put as an entrance to the kitchen garden. The house itself had a more prim Victorian front and the grey austerity of the typical Lakeland farm. The back of it was centuries older. There were kitchens with great flagged stone floors and doors of vast oak made without benefit of nails. The kitchen had probably been one great room in the earliest stage of the house. There was an impression in the ceiling which marked where a hole used to be kept open to let the smoke escape from a fire in the middle of the floor—the usual place for one before fireplaces were invented. The house had most likely been one of the great farms founded by the Viking invaders, of whom there are still many traces in place-names such as Grisdale (the Dale of the Pigs) and the local use of the word 'til' for 'to'.

The house had the interesting name of High Cross, and we felt somehow drawn to it. We were most disappointed therefore when the farmer's wife, Mrs Fearon, told us she was unable to take us in.

After that we went to innumerable other houses, but entirely without success. Some weeks later when still searching we happened to meet a neighbour in the lane, a Quaker schoolmaster, and when we spoke of our problem he remarked, without apparently having any practical reason to do so, 'I think Mrs Fearon will take you in.'

After he had passed on we began to think his remark over. He was a man of few and accurate words. What had made him say it? She lived at the other end of the village and they never met. Had he somehow been used to relay to us unconsciously something that they on the Other Side wished to say? We went back to High Cross. Directly Mrs Fearon opened the door we saw that her attitude to us had changed. We explained to her that we were now vegetarians and ate mostly salads, and what little cooking was necessary we could manage on our small oil stoves in the sitting-room. When she heard she could keep her kitchen to herself she at once agreed to our coming.

We moved in a few days later. As we did so Gladys had a remarkable experience. She saw on the doorstep the same young girl who had appeared to her in her friend's drive at Grasmere. She appeared to be very close to Mrs Fearon, as if she was overshadowing her and helping and influencing her for good. When Gladys mentioned this Mrs Fearon said that she had lost a beloved little daughter, Margaret, when she was eighteen months old. Gladys said this was Margaret who had grown up in the spirit world. To corroborate this she said that soon after Margaret died an uncle had suffered a violent death. Margaret also brought with her an elderly lady who died of a disease in the stomach, whom Mrs Fearon had helped very much.

Mrs Fearon was able to corroborate all these statements. Her husband's brother was killed on the line two weeks after Margaret died and Mrs Fearon herself had looked after an old aunt and nursed her when she was dying of cancer of the stomach.

This sudden revelation from the Unseen world must have seemed strange to a farmer's wife living a quiet country life, but Mrs Fearon seemed to assimilate it at once quite easily and a great friendship grew between her and Gladys. Though they were very different in thought and background, none of the strains and stresses came between them which might have done between landlady and lodger. For instance, Mrs Fearon felt that, as she put it, 'cats should never be ornaments', they should be workers, and she had the conventional farmer's idea that they should be given the minimum of food as they were to catch the rats. Gladys was very fond of cats and had quite different ideas about them. The cats soon got to know this and all appeared at her window or slid in through the door to her sitting-room, where they regaled themselves on the fat of the land. But nothing critical was said about it by Mrs Fearon, and it became obvious that there was some deeper link between Gladys and Mrs Fearon which had come about before this comparatively short meeting at High Cross in our present age.

At a sitting in the October after we settled at High Cross some interesting observations were made about our connections there. The sitting began with a most unusual announcement:

> There are some Guides here, standing over there, they belong to you and Ralph and Daddy [Feda said]. They will be helping later, Guides from the East, Guides and Teachers and I feel they are here to help Ralph with what he wants to say about this.
>
> You were brought here to this part. You wonder how and why. He knows. Wait, wait, wait!
>
> He says Gladys was inclined to think that it was the man with the house by the water who made the link [a reference to the husband of one of Gladys's sitters who lived near by]. No there are far stronger links with us all three. This man only made use of it. This place has associations with you long ago. There are certain things we don't often talk to you about, sometimes it is unwise, sometimes we can't, things we have knowledge of on our own plane which have no relationship to events in our earth life. Now those are the things it is difficult to reconstruct mentally in a sitting. I am not in my normal condition now, this condition is something to which I am adjusting myself for the purpose of talking to you; but I would say that there is only a percentage of my conscious mind and memory here. There are things I know about you, all three of you on my plane, that go, or partly go, when I am in touch with the earth conditions. Conditions are denser,

> consciousness does not function so well here. This should be more widely known in the movement. That is why we remember some things and not others. You sometimes say 'How strange he recalled that but did not say so-and-so which was much more important.' That was because I could not reconstruct it in this atmosphere.

Feda then relayed a message from Margaret Fearon, stating that we had all been on earth together before in a former life. Her mother had not progressed as far as Margaret had, so she had come back as a child to make a link. She praised her mother's devotion to duty in her present work as a farmer's wife, but begged us to tell her about the things of the spirit that she might progress in this knowledge especially.

Perhaps this statement by Feda was further enhanced by a visual experience Gladys had one day when paying a visit to Mrs Fearon in the old kitchen. Suddenly she saw her standing there, clad in long robes, of a past age, looking very dignified.

Mrs Fearon, knowing nothing of this, one day made the quite unexpected remark to Gladys, 'Well sometimes you feel links that make you think you have met a person before, it seems the only way of explaining it doesn't it?'

We tried to carry out Margaret's instructions and help Mrs Fearon to open out on these things. We were fairly successful because she seemed very interested and sympathetic. She never made any difficulty about having Gladys's sitters to the house, though it must at first have seemed very strange to her to have people coming for such a purpose. The friendship that grew between her and Gladys long outlasted our stay there. After we left they corresponded as often as their busy lives would allow.

It was, however, only some years after we had left and I went back to Loweswater alone on a holiday that the full explanation of all this became apparent, the last pieces fitting, as it were, into the jigsaw puzzle.

It was so good to be back there. I went delightedly up the long drive with its avenue of trees. High Cross was a place of distinctive personality. It did not let you forget it. I got no reply at the front door, but I was not surprised as Mrs Fearon was usually busy at the back of the house. I passed through the iron gates at the side and into the kitchen garden. From here a winding path led to the back door. I knocked there, but there was no reply. I looked round, and in the far corner of the garden I saw a figure bending over a fork, digging up vegetables. I went over there and saw it was Joe, Mrs Fearon's youngest son. I greeted him and said, 'I came to see your mother, but I can't find her.' He straightened himself up for a moment and then I saw that his eyes were full of tears.

'My mother,' he said, 'died suddenly two weeks ago, from a stroke.'

Then I realized the meaning of Margaret's mission, why she had found Gladys out and followed her to Loweswater, and impressed Mrs Fearon finally to take us in. She knew that her mother's time in this earthly life was not long, so she had wanted to do everything she could to help her to learn about the spiritual life and make her ready to enter the next world. It is amazing how one can trace a pattern and purpose in the way events happen.

This is the kind of thing that leads me to feel that psychic knowledge and guidance is not merely a playback of the sitter's mind, but an intelligent communication made after consideration and thought on the part of someone who has a greater knowledge than our limited vision allows, and who can see the problem in relation to the distant past and future. Therefore it is our duty to co-operate with them in carrying out their purpose. It helps both them and us.

High Cross was a strange house for bringing back memories, and probably a powerhouse for making communications possible from the past. I had an experience myself there which I have always remembered with interest, though it was not conclusive enough to be put down as evidence. In a dream one night I saw the back of the house, and was surprised to find that the whole farmyard, which I knew only as a muddy morass encircled by cow sheds, was covered in green grass and even had some flowers in it. I could not unfortunately bring back very much detail. Some days later I was writing a letter to a friend in India who had written a novel about reincarnation and who therefore had links with this subject. I was describing the house, and directly I came to write about the back of it I felt I was hurtling back in a strange way to the dream of a few days before. Too excited, I tried to grasp its details too quickly for my normal consciousness. Just as Ralph had said he found in sittings, it slipped out of my reach.

I was very interested, much later, when reading the famous historical novel *Kristin Lavransdatter* to discover a historical note by the author, Sigrid Undset, stating that the courtyards of the great Norwegian farms were always covered with greensward. I have seen this myself when visiting the folk museums of Norway with their detailed reconstructions of the environs of the great farms. This was an entirely alien conception of a farmyard to me, who had been brought up in the bleak north of England where farmyards were a sea of mud for most of the year. So such a picture was certainly not in my mind.

Cumberland, the county in which High Cross is situated, is of course rich in Norse relics. Almost every large and very old farm is said to have originated as a Viking settlement.

I often used to go out of High Cross and stand on a knoll at the side looking through the iron gates and over the kitchen garden to the lower slopes of the fells beyond. Here there was a gap in between two of the lesser mountains, and so somehow I always felt a feeling of anticipation as if, at any moment, some people might come riding out of the pass, and they would be very important to me.

Could it be that this strange glimpse of the back of the house covered in greensward had some link with a past life here with Gladys and Mrs Fearon, and could this account for my deep love of Norway, for which I have never otherwise been able to account.

Another curious dream experience had occurred to me many years ago as a child in a completely different place, long before I knew High Cross, but it was so vivid that I still recall it clearly. When I begin to consider this I realize how strangely it links with the Cumberland experience, in spite of its entirely different time and place.

I dreamt that I walked along a path in our familiar kitchen garden, of which I was particularly fond. When I came to the wall of the barn which backed on to it I saw that the shutter, covering a round hole in the wall where the hay was put into the loft, was open.

I peeped in and viewed with horror a strange man dressed in some kind of armour with a helmet on his head which had some spread-eagled design like wings on it. He was deeply asleep in the hay, snoring heavily. I listened petrified for some moments. As I stole away I knew that he had somehow all at once come to stay there and life could never be the same again, never free from terror so long as he sojourned with us. I felt his presence as something new and more acutely terrifying than anything we had ever had to face before. The dream was so vivid I have never forgotten it. Could it be some memory of a Viking invasion in Cumberland in a past childhood? (I have so often read later how they slept in the barns.) Could it have made such a deep emotional impression on me that it had imprinted itself indelibly on my personality? The fact that it is so connected with my impressions at High Cross does seem to substantiate such a conclusion.

16

New work and the future

When we had made the link with Mrs Fearon and conveyed to her what Margaret wished, the way was opened for us to return to Jordans.

Ralph had said in a sitting about twelve weeks before, 'There may be a chance for you to return south soon.' And in another he warned us, 'We may move you suddenly so be prepared.'

In the late autumn a wire came from Mrs Brant, in whose house we had first stayed at Jordans, saying there was a small house to let furnished on the Green. Would we take it?

After some cogitation we wired back an acceptance of the offer. Strangely enough the house was called Little Haven. Mrs Leonard's home at Tankerton was called The Haven so we thought this was a good omen. It was, for the house proved to be a wonderful haven for the rest of the war years.

We left High Cross sadly, for in some ways we had put down deep roots there, but life was growing hard with the bleak part of the winter coming on. Paraffin, our chief means of heat and light, was so short that we had to go to bed by about 9.30 because we dared not keep our stove or lamp burning longer.

We had to leave High Cross at about 6 a.m. to drive to Penrith to catch almost the only train that went south in the day. Under war conditions, of course, it all had to be done in complete darkness because of the blackout. We were not only encumbered with all our luggage and the various domestic paraphernalia we seemed to have acquired from six months of living in rooms, but also with a precious cat in a basket. This was Dodie, a small but very important member of the cat colony at High Cross whom we had decided, on account of her frailty and thinness, could not be left behind to fight the hard battle of a farm cat's life. I was not to know then of the important part even she would play in our psychic revelations, and which I have described in Chapter 8. We should also have brought Aunt Jane, an old dark tabby who had so urgently solicited our care we could not bear to leave her either. But she was very deaf and had been killed by the grocer's lorry, which she had failed to see entering the yard just a few days before we moved south. She is immortalized in Mrs Leonard's book *Brief Darkness* which was written while living at High Cross and which was published by Cassell after we returned to Jordans.

The strength of the cat basket which friends kindly provided for Dodie proved quite inadequate for her thin, snaky little body. Never having been in a basket before, she became extremely restless and soon demolished the bottom. As we were passing over the wild moorland known as Shapp on the main road between England and the Scotch border, we felt her sliding about among us like an elusive snake in the darkness. It was a terrifying experience, for we did not dare put on the light to catch her for fear of enemy planes. As fast as we blindly grabbed hold of a bit of her she wriggled free again. We feared that she might find a gap in a window or somewhere else in the car and escape into the barren wildness of the moor, where, in December, she would not long have survived.

We arrived somehow at Penrith station to find to our alarm we were late. The train was already coming in on the other side of the station. It was the only one of the day, so we *must* get it. Somehow a kindly porter produced a bag, and instead of putting the cat in it, as I think he intended, we put the basket in the bag so that it provided a bottom and somehow held it together.

Staggering along with our various bits of luggage we just made the train. We fell into a first-class carriage as it was all that was empty. Gladys turned very sick with the strain of it all, and had to be given brandy. When the ticket collector saw all this, he let us remain where we were on our third-class tickets instead of compelling us to pay or stand in the corridor. So we travelled in luxury! Like most war-time trains it was absolutely packed.

We were therefore very thankful to reach our peaceful Little Haven after a car, which met us at Watford, had driven us across country to our new house.

Ralph's advice, given in a sitting at Jordans before we left for the Lake District, had proved quite right. He had advised me not to take work with the Quakers outside London, but to wait till later, when I should get something 'on the spot', as he put it. By apparent chance I received a letter from a Norwegian friend, an exile in London, saying he had been invited to a conference at the Quaker College of Woodbroke to discuss plans for an international centre they were setting up in London. I wrote at once to the Society of Friends offering to do voluntary service there and was accepted. This fitted in exactly with our return to Jordans. It is interesting that, as with the bungalow in the Lakes, it was yet another Norwegian link that gave me the clue to another important plan in my life and helped me to make my offer at the right time.

These Quaker Embassies, as Carl Heath, their founder, named them, were already established in several countries throughout the world. They provided unique centres where people of different nations and points of view could really get to know one another and understand in depth the problems of each country or minority. They were staffed by members of different nations and had a population of residential guests as well as those who came in for the many meetings arranged in the programmes.

The war created a unique opportunity to make this scheme of particular value. It brought to London the 'shadow cabinets' of innumerable nations. Here, on neutral territory belonging to the non-combatant Quakers, everyone could meet and talk freely. There were people of every creed and colour, or of no creed at all. They represented all strata of a nation, from young students to exiled ministers of state.

There were special national study groups as well as the chance to mix with other nationalities in the lounge, and there were more general lectures which all nationals attended together, concerts and lunch-time talks on current affairs with questions and discussion afterwards. I remember one highly amusing occasion when Barbara Ward came to the centre. She was of Catholic and Quaker parentage. She had given a brilliant disquisition on current affairs and the chairman asked if there were any questions. A stocky little German atheist shot to his feet and said, 'Yes, I would like to ask what plans Miss Ward's God has made should the Allies be defeated.'

Needless to say, it had not been a talk based on cheap patriotism but one couched in the brilliant logic of all her speeches, and so everyone enjoyed the joke and a fitting reply was easily supplied by the speaker.

My own work at first was mainly in the background, doing domestic work, as not myself belonging to the Society of Friends, I had felt I should volunteer for any kind of work to get the opportunity to work there. Able to look on from the background, I learnt a great deal that was valuable.

In a sitting at Jordans soon after I started at the centre Ralph suddenly said:

> Don't be disappointed if there are some difficulties to do with changes with regard to your work at the centre. Whatever you do don't get hurt or cross about anything and leave, because you have got to stay there in order to meet a man who will give you some really important work you are meant to do.

Forewarned is forearmed, and so I bore this in mind when, quite soon after, it was decided that I was really redundant. My work could be done by a daily woman from the neighbourhood. It was first suggested that I should be asked to leave. I did not appear hurt, but just sat quietly thinking of Ralph's words. Before any final decision was taken, however, the whole committee had to discuss the matter. Two members then put forward a suggestion that a new job should be created for me. I was to be on duty each day in the lounge on the ground floor to receive and help the sundry people who came through their ever-open door. This was, of course, a job after my own heart. It gave me some scope for my social science training and satisfied my wish to make contact with members of other nations and to understand their viewpoints.

My hours were to be from 10 in the morning till 5.30. Hitherto I had been staying late into the evening. The change gave me an extraordinary sense of freedom, so I decided to try and form a study group on Norway. I only envisaged that we might bring together a group of English people who were specially interested in that country who planned to try and go there to do relief work once the war was over. I knew few Norwegians in London at that time, and did not expect that we should attract many. They would hardly want to come to hear about their own country since they knew about it already. I forgot how they were a people in exile, and hence would long to hear about familiar things again and mingle with a sympathetic group of English people who also wanted to hear about their country.

There was no difficulty in obtaining speakers. When the warden of the centre heard of my plan, he took me straight to Kingston House, a huge block of flats in Kensington, occupied mainly by the Norwegian government offices. Here we met the Prime Minister's secretary, Miss Ragna Hagen—a vital and original personality who was to become a very good friend. Through her and the help of the Information Office a whole panel of speakers was shortly arranged. We started with the well-known Mayor of Narvik, Theodor Broch, who had escaped across the Swedish frontier after twice being condemned to death. He was just publishing his remarkable book about his experiences *The Mountains Wait.*

The first meeting was small, but once the news went round in earnest the Norwegians poured in. My mother came to help by making huge pots of strong coffee, which was consumed in vast quantities. On one occasion the speaker, a Norwegian professor, phoned to say he would be late as he was being kept in Bristol by the Ministry of Supply. Could we wait for him? I said yes. He was two hours late, but all the time we continued to lay on coffee and the audience kept drinking it and talking and appearing to be perfectly happy. By this stage I was feeling rather stern and fully intended to show my disapproval, since this professor had cancelled a previous lecture altogether. When at last he did arrive I came out of a room off the hall and I ran into him suddenly, never having met him before. Encountering his blue-eyed smile and hearing his profound apologies in irresistible, soft Norwegian tones, how could I be cross? No one who came from a country like Norway, experiencing hazardous journeys across mountains and other delaying obstacles, could be expected to be tied down to a precise programme. I had to take this into consideration.

The meeting was a roaring success and I came to count the

professor as one of my many good friends from Norway. In fact it was he, I believe, who recommended me for the longed-for post with the Norwegians which Ralph had foretold would be offered if I stayed put to meet this man at the centre.

With Gladys safely ensconced in Little Haven we began a little Sunday-night circle with our friends with whom we had first lived in the village, and here the pattern of Norwegian events was revealed. During one session Mrs Brant got a remarkable precognition concerning Norway, though we could not then identify it.

One evening, when concentrating, she suddenly exclaimed:

> Oh, I see a big white ship laden with relief supplies and refugees and it is going back somewhere up a waterway bounded by rocks that come down to the water. There is a bright sunshine and the people on the boat are very happy. On the quay I see a man in a peaked cap leaning on a rail, round him there is a very dark shadow.

At the end of the war the famous cruising ship *Andes* was diverted from carrying Allied Air Force personnel to the Far East and lent to the Norwegians to take the government and civilians back in one huge party. Hundreds of exiles went home on her. By no mere coincidence, our doctor friend David, in whose house we had lived at Highgate at the beginning of the war, was the doctor on board. He was able to give us an eye-witness account of the journey. The weather, he said, had been brilliant, and as they steamed up Oslo Fjord the sunlight fell so dazzlingly on the ship that, although it was painted war-time grey like all ships then, it really looked like its original white in the sharp northern light. When we returned to Norway and sought out old friends, we found that one, a sailor who had been forced to remain, had suffered some very tragic things. He was the man in the shadow in the peaked cap.

Speaking in July 1942 Ralph had said:

> Germany will have some bad kicks to give before cracking up, but then everything will meet at a point and collapse.

Certainly this was exactly what happened when Berlin fell and Hitler and most members of the Nazi hierarchy either died by their own hands or survived to face judgement at the Nuremberg Trials. The railway train of my dream, having zigzagged like the real military campaigns across Europe and Africa, had truly come to the edge of a precipice and been forced to a standstill, and we, the terrified passengers, were to our amazement still safe and sound, despite its mad career. Symbolically, we had in the end indeed reached Newcastle, as I heard my brother's voice say in the dream.

What about the other aspect of his statement? Had I really reached the gateway to Norway? There was a strange lull once the tension of war in Europe ceased. We lived in limbo for a time while the exiles were caught up in the excitement of return.

I began to doubt Ralph's forecast. I struggled to keep up my Norwegian links, but they seemed to diminish.

There was a terrible landslide in our friends when the *Andes* sailed. London felt so empty without them. It seemed as if my work for the Norwegians had come to an end. But I kept in mind the fact that Ralph had told me that I should find an important opening to do with my work when on going to a place quite unexpectedly and not with that end in mind at all. I waited patiently, trusting that, since the other things had worked out, this one might too.

A Norwegian girl came to stay with us through friends. She had got into some difficulty through having several unsatisfactory jobs. Quite without any thought of what it might lead to later, I took her to see the Cultural Attaché, who had recently arrived and set up his office in Norway's new embassy premises in Belgrave Square, to see if he could help. When he heard my name he was delighted.

'Well, I have been wanting to get in touch with you,' he exclaimed. 'It has been suggested in Oslo that you should be asked to take on the honorary secretaryship of the Anglo-Norse Society!' Of course I accepted immediately. At a meeting on 27 May my name was put forward and I was duly elected.

This happened on the eve of my first visit to Norway after the war. I decided for various reasons, including ones of economy, to travel by ship from Newcastle, and so went there in the physical sense as well as the symbolic, just as my dream had shown.

Having had a happy reunion with Norway and my friends, I returned to England, and in the autumn, when everyone else was back from their holidays, we began the work of building up our membership for the Anglo-Norse Society.

Dr Wilhelmsen, the Cultural Attaché, most generously accommodated me in the embassy library with his secretary and librarian. Even he himself had to work in there at first, as the decorators were in his office. But I was made most welcome, and what an amusing time we had all together. I had at last really become part of the Norway I loved so well. A friend from the B.B.C. laughed at me one day when I introduced him at an embassy party to '*our* Counsellor'. He had to remind me that I was not a Norwegian subject, a fact I had forgotten. I felt so essentially part of the community that I worked in I remained honorary secretary for about fifteen years. I am still a member of the Anglo-Norse Council in London.

Now I can see how the whole jigsaw came to fit, the wisdom of Ralph's guidance, his plea for patience in the changeover at the International Centre, the injunction not to leave till I had met the man who would make the link with the next task I had to fulfil. And the culmination—the opening of the gateway to Norway—illustrated the final fulfilment of those words of his which had kept me going through all the black years of the war, '*All will be well* and you will get to Newcastle in the end.'

I have sought to underline these events because I feel that it is by such an awareness to clues, such a discipline in waiting for the right moment to act, that we keep to our particular road and find the path in which we are to live our fullest and best.

Looking back over the wider horizon, these messages have indicated an apparently destined path of development in the world, which is undoubtedly taken care of by divine providence. Even though man may stray from his intended direction, the pattern underlying the whole appears to work itself out.

It was right back in the 1930s that Ralph had first spoken of the interesting and unusual things I should see coming to pass in my lifetime on earth. In 1931 he spoke of how those in the After Life were drawing near in order to begin their special work of impressing the earth. In later years he forecast that the coming in of the new age would be marked by riots and unrest, world war and dark times. He also forecast many squabbles in the post-war period over how to construct the new world. He looked on all these, however, not as sources of despair but as the birth-pangs of a new age.

In spite of these tragedies, the world was moving in the direction that God intended. 'When this cloud has passed,' he said, 'we shall establish with you a new world order.'

Much of this appears to have come to pass. Man's whole attitude and way of life has altered over the past years through influences coming from many directions. The discovery of atomic power has changed his whole conception of war and his attitude to peace. The possibilities of atomic power for peaceful uses has opened up vast new fields of development. The production of man-made materials, nylon furs and plant protein, have taken the emphasis off killing right down as far as the animal kingdom.

In the international field we have watched the rapid comings and goings of national leaders thousands of miles across the world when crisis creates a necessity to confer. We have seen the devoted efforts of new world citizens like Dag Hammarskjöld and U Thant to keep the peace through the United Nations. We have watched the great powers come to the very edge of the abyss of self-destruction during the Cuba crisis, but by some miracle and our altered attitude to war have seen the clouds of conflict clear and the ships with their atomic missiles go home.

Since then we have seen the small peace movements widen into vast anti-war organizations bringing together thousands of people of every point of view to back the great world-wide opinion that war must be stopped.

Vast changes have come in other mental spheres too: altered views on human relationships, growing tolerance between the world's churches and religions. New fields in the study of the deeper consciousness and extra-sensory perception have been opened, bringing nearer the final part of Ralph's forecast.

It is in this sphere that Ralph's last and most intriguing prophecy must be, perhaps I should say is being, fulfilled. Speaking of these things in previous years, Ralph has said:

Such interesting things will happen [in the future]. We are only on the verge of the very beginning. We hope it won't be long before we are able to come through to you in a more direct and better way.

In a later record he explained:

I am trying to learn how to get through to you myself so that you will know I am there. I shall never be satisfied until I have done it. No one knows much about it on our side or yours but when you come over you will be another one to explain what puzzles you and what seems difficult to you on earth.

We shall get through to you in a way that you will see and hear us objectively, not hope we are there, not think we are there, but I feel you will see, hear and touch us.

We also received the interesting observation, 'If you go and live in a special place you could see us, one where there is not the present wear and tear—that is *in time*.' The latter words were stressed in the direct voice to emphasize their importance of, I suppose, a gradual sensitizing achieved through perseverance.

My father then joined in the conversation and said:

In time you will make conditions on this earth, even in this country by isolating places when this subject is more understood. Just as people now buy up villages or estates you will, and turn them into Sanctuaries and safeguard them. They will be kept as special spaces for contacting the Other Side. In time he is sure that will be done [Feda added].

We seem to have been given some further clues regarding this process when Feda talked of our friend Walter's appearance at Malta, about which I wrote further back. It was emphasized that this was an objective seeing, not clairvoyance. He explained how something building up, verging on both worlds, a certain steadiness in the atmosphere, thoughts having been sent out strongly, may all help to build up something to come sufficiently from the etheric to the physical stage to enable it to become visible to us. The shell of the etheric has slipped over your world as it were.

This is the part we are only on the verge of. On 24 January 1966 Mrs Osborne Leonard sent for me because she said she felt that our friends in the Other World had something they wanted to say to me. This came as a great surprise, as she had retired from her professional work as a trance medium some years before and she seldom got messages for me when not in trance.

When I arrived at The Haven, at Tankerton, she said, 'I feel that they want me to say that in the future you will be hearing of people having a lot of strange experiences which may be very important. I cannot quite get the full meaning of this.'

Recalling our previous messages I understood well what our friends meant. This, I told her, must indicate the beginning of the final stage that Ralph spoke of in his forecast of the new age.

She accepted this and was very pleased to hear of its significance, because as a deep-trance medium she had no knowledge of the material we obtained in our sittings, so it was not in her conscious thoughts.

Soon afterwards I began to hear of many people having strange experiences, and these seem to have increased as time has gone on. To add to this there is this great interest among people, especially the young, in meditation and wider concepts of the superconscious reflected in an additional interest in press and TV and other expressions of mass media. Through this many people may discover unrealized gifts: Rosemary Brown, for instance, who has brought through new work from great composers on the Other Side of Life.

To add to this there are scientific developments: the discovery of higher frequencies in telephonic communications, and such visual perceptions as radar. All are moving towards the whole uncovering of the great Unseen.

Soon after her passing to the After Life in 1968 Gladys Osborne Leonard came back to me through a new medium who had never known her and who was unaware of her or my identity. She was accompanied by a bearded man, who, the medium said, was very pleased to link up with her again over there (presumably Sir Oliver Lodge).

'I want to tell you,' she said emphatically, 'that the great breakthrough *is* coming.'

Let us look to the future, therefore, and be prepared for it in order to realize in a disciplined and constructive way the opportunities it will present.